John's Guide to *Ulysses*

By

John Salinsky

Published by New Generation Publishing in 2022

Copyright © John Salinsky 2022

First Edition

The author asserts the moral right under the Copyright, Designs and Patents Act 1988 to be identified as the author of this work.

All Rights reserved. No part of this publication may be reproduced, stored in a retrieval system or transmitted, in any form or by any means without the prior consent of the author, nor be otherwise circulated in any form of binding or cover other than that which it is published and without a similar condition being imposed on the subsequent purchaser.

ISBN   978-1-80369-387-3

www.newgeneration-publishing.com

New Generation Publishing

Contents

WHICH EDITION OF ULYSSES?........................i

A BIOGRAPHY OF JAMES JOYCE (1882 -1941) ii

READING ULYSSES: a beginner's guide............ v

ULYSSES: THE EPISODES................................xi

PART I 1

   Notes on Episode 1: TELEMACHUS (pages 1-28). 2

   Notes on Episode 2: NESTOR (28-45) 8

   Notes on Episode 3: PROTEUS (45-64) 11

PART II.. 16

   Notes on Episode 4: CALYPSO (65-85).......... 17

   Notes on Episode 5: LOTUS-EATERS (85-107) 22

   Notes on Episode 6: HADES (107-147)........... 26

   Notes on Episode 7: AEOLUS (147-189) 33

   Notes on Episode 8: LESTRYGONIANS (190-234).. 40

   Notes on Episode 9: SCYLLA AND CHARYBDIS (235-280) 45

   Notes on Episode 10: WANDERING ROCKS (280-328) 51

   Notes on Episode 11: SIRENS (328 - 376) 60

Notes on Episode 12: CYCLOPS (376-449).... 66

Notes on Episode 13: NAUSICAA (449-499). 75

Notes on Episode 14: OXEN OF THE SUN (499-561) 82

Notes on Episode 15: CIRCE (561-703) 95

PART III 112

Notes on Episode 16: EUMAEUS (704 -776) 113

Notes on Episode 17: ITHACA Part 1 (776-819) 121

Notes on Episode 17A: ITHACA, part two (819 - 871) 127

Notes on Episode 18: PENELOPE (871-933) 135

WHICH EDITION OF ULYSSES?

There is a new (2022) Penguin Vintage edition, but I am afraid I don't like it. The print is tiny and smudgy and the whole book is difficult to handle. The text contains 'corrections' of about 5000 words, proposed by Hans Walter Gabler after some long and intensive study of the manuscripts. Not everyone liked his version and there was a controversy among the Joyce scholars until Gabler's version was eventually accepted for use by academics and students.

None of Gabler's changes make any difference to ordinary readers like ourselves.

My preferred edition for us is the **Penguin Classics paperback** which has larger print and is very easy to read and to handle (despite its size). So you will find that all my page references in the Guide are to this edition.

If you do choose a different one, you will still be able to find the references as you read, but it might take a little longer.

A BIOGRAPHY OF JAMES JOYCE (1882 -1941)

James was the oldest surviving child of John Stanislaus Joyce and May Joyce (nee Murray), then living in the Dublin suburb of Rathgar. They subsequently had 9 more children. The family frequently had to move as a result of the father's growing inability to support them after he lost his only regular job as a rate collector.

At the age of seven, James was sent to Clongowes Wood College, a Jesuit boarding school in county Kildare. When his father could no longer afford the fees, he was sent to the Christian Brothers school and then to another Jesuit school, Belvedere College. He did well at school and won several prizes; he also had a religious crisis and abandoned his Christian faith, (though it continued to haunt him). Nonetheless, when he graduated from Belvedere, he entered University College, Dublin, another Jesuit institution. His academic and literary gifts were soon recognised as was his critical attitudes to the church, and to Irish society's failure to mobilise itself and work effectively towards Independence from England. However, he was well liked because of his sense of humour and his good tenor voice. As a student, he also had an impressive knowledge of literature both English and European.

In 1902 he was awarded his degree in modern languages. He immediately left Dublin for Paris where he intended to study medicine but did not persevere with it for long. In April 1903, he was summoned home because his mother was seriously ill and she died in August, a few months later.

Joyce then stayed in Dublin and started writing the short stories which would eventually be published as

Dubliners. During this time he was a teacher in a school in Dalkey (see episode 2 of *Ulysses*) and spent a week living in the Sandycove Martello Tower with his friend Oliver St John Gogarty. His time there appears in fictionalised form in the first episode of *Ulysses* ('Telemachus').

On 10 June 1904, he met Nora Barnacle and went on a date with her for the first time on 16 June, which he commemorated as the day on which *Ulysses* is set. After a few months he and Nora left Dublin and settled in Trieste where James supported them by giving English lessons. He finished *Dubliners*, wrote a collection of poems (*Chamber Music*), and started work on a semi-autobiographical novel, eventually published in 1916 as *A Portrait of the Artist as a Young Man.* In this book, his hero, Stephen Dedalus, is clearly recognisable as Joyce himself as a child and later as a student. In 1914 he also started to write *Ulysses,* in which a slightly older version of Stephen (aged 22) is one of the principal characters.

The Joyces had two children, Giorgio and Lucia. Lucia unhappily developed schizophrenia and lived most of her adult life in a psychiatric hospital in England. James visited Dublin several times between 1909 and 1912, but never for long. When the First World War broke out, the family moved to Zurich and after the war they settled in Paris. By this time Joyce had won the admiration of a number of eminent writers including W B Yeats and Ezra Pound who were able to get him some much needed financial support. But he was always short of money.

The early chapters of *Ulysses* were published by an American literary magazine, The Little Review, and aroused a great deal of interest. However, in 1920, publication was stopped as a result of a prosecution on the grounds that *Ulysses* was pornographic. Or, at least, it contained sexual material which was deemed unacceptable in print. Joyce continued writing new chapters and the complete book was eventually published in 1922 by Sylvia Beach who ran an English language bookshop in Paris called Shakespeare and Co. An American edition was subsequently interrupted on the same grounds and the book was also banned in England, though not in Ireland, although it was hard to obtain. *Ulysses* was finally cleared of these charges by an American Court in 1933. It was first available in England in 1937.

Joyce had meanwhile started working on his last and even more complex novel, *Finnegans Wake*, which was published in 1939. His eyesight had begun to deteriorate progressively in the 1930s and he was also increasingly preoccupied with the problem of his daughter's mental illness. When the Second World War started, the Joyces moved back to Paris where James died in 1941, at the age of 59, from a perforated duodenal ulcer.

READING *ULYSSES*: a beginner's guide

Ulysses was written by James Joyce, an Irish writer who lived most of his life in continental Europe (Trieste, Zurich and Paris). In these three cities most of the book was written between 1914 and 1922.

When it was published in 1922 it changed the world of literature forever.

What is *Ulysses* about?

The story is set on a single day, June 16th 1904 in the city of Dublin. (Actually, there is an overlap till well after 2 a.m. next morning.)

The main characters you will meet are:

Stephen Dedalus, an aspiring young writer in his early twenties. He is very intense and tends to brood a good deal about how he can fulfil his potential as an artist. He is rather like the young James Joyce.

Leopold Bloom, a 38 year old Jewish man. Well, half Jewish, through his Jewish father. He is a modest, good-natured representative of the common man. And yet he is in many ways unusual. He is observant and intensely curious, with a very rich inner life, which we readers are privileged to share. He has a rather humble job selling advertisements to newspapers. Everyone seems to know him, but he is regarded as an outsider and an oddity by most people. The men tend to make fun of him; although one acquaintance concedes that '*there's a touch of the artist about old Bloom.*' And, the better we get to know him, the more complex his inner life seems to be.

Molly Bloom. Molly is Leopold's attractive, very sexy wife. She is also a semi-professional singer, with a good soprano voice. The other Dubliners can't understand how a nobody like Bloom can have such a desirable wife, and they are rather envious. The Blooms have a 15-year-old daughter (Milly). Sadly, their second child, a little boy called Rudolf (Rudy), died at the age of 11 days, 11 years ago. Since then, their sex life has been, to say the least, incomplete; though both have sex on their mind a good deal and Molly, while faithful in her fashion, is about to have an affair as the story opens. Molly has the last chapter of *Ulysses* all to herself and she uses it to tell us all about what it's like (for her), to be a woman.

The plot. Stephen and Bloom wander separately round Dublin. Their paths cross at various points. Meanwhile, Molly is going to entertain a new lover in her bedroom. Bloom rescues Stephen from a potentially violent encounter in the Dublin red light district and takes him home for a cup of cocoa.

Is Bloom looking for a lost son and Stephen for a more supportive father? Maybe. Mr Bloom is a thoughtful observer of everything he sees during the day. But his thoughts keep returning anxiously to Molly's infidelity which will happen at 4 p.m.

Surely, there must be more to it than that?

Of course there is! There are all sorts of adventures along the way and we get to know all the main characters well. Some will become friends for life.

Why is *Ulysses* widely regarded as a difficult (even impossible) book to read?

Some of it is extremely difficult! But much of it is very easy and enjoyable. Joyce writes in an astonishing variety of different ways, sometimes changing from the everyday to the obscure and allusive, or back again, from one paragraph to the next. There is a good deal of brilliant parody of different literary styles. For much of the time he uses the 'interior monologue' method in which everything that goes through a character's mind is immediately available. It's like sitting inside someone's head. Amazing!

There are lots of jokes and puns some of which you won't get at first. Other passages will make you laugh out loud and think: how come this is supposed to be a very serious book?

It is a very clever book, full of allusions and puzzles; but it's also full of warm regard for humanity. And you will come across phrases that are so poetic they will make you tingle with pleasure.

Finally, it is a very musical book. Several 'theme songs' are repeatedly quoted or referred to throughout the text. The most notable of these are the 'seduction' duet, 'La ci darem in mano' ('Put your hand in mine') from Mozart's *Don Giovanni*, and the popular Victorian ballad, 'Love's old sweet song'. Both of these are on Molly's mind (and her husband's), as she will be singing them in her forthcoming concert tour, promoted by the lecherous Hugh 'Blazes' Boylan. Much of the text has a musical sound when read aloud and one chapter (Sirens), is written as if it was a musical composition.

Why is it called *Ulysses*?

Joyce said that the book was a kind of modern day version of *The Odyssey,* the epic ancient Greek poem by Homer. *The Odyssey* is the sequel to Homer's *The Iliad.* It tells the story of the adventures of the Greek general, Odysseus (Roman name, Ulysses), on his long-delayed journey home from the Trojan War.

However, the story does not follow the same chronology as *The Odyssey* and the characters have only a little in common with their Homeric originals.

There are all sorts of references to *The Odyssey*, which keep the scholars busy. It is absolutely ***not necessary*** to pick all these up to understand and appreciate *Ulysses*.

The structure of *Ulysses*

The chapters *in Ulysses* are not named or even numbered. They are referred to as 'Episodes' each of which represents an episode in Homer's Odyssey. There is just a break with a horizontal line at the end of each one.

Joyce originally put in chapter names corresponding to episodes in Homer's *Odyssey*. But then, having told all his friends the names, he removed them! However, all Joyceans refer to the episodes by these names, and we shall do likewise. You will soon get to know them.

There are **18 episodes** arranged in **three sections** (numbered I, II and III) with three, twelve and three episodes respectively.

The **first section** is all about **Stephen Dedalus**, a young man full of artistic aspirations (and self-doubt).

The **middle section** of twelve episodes introduces **Leopold Bloom** who features in most of them, making brief appearances in all the others.

The **last section** brings Bloom and Stephen together and the final episode is entirely given over to **Molly Bloom**.

Each episode is set at a particular hour of the day. These run chronologically from 8 a.m. to 2 a.m. the following morning. Except that, when the middle section begins with the introduction of Leopold Bloom, we go back to 8 a.m.

Joyce helpfully provided his friends with a plan showing the time and place of each episode. He also let them know that each episode had its own organ of the body, art, colour, symbol and 'technic'.

These were originally set out by Stuart Gilbert who wrote one of the early commentaries on *Ulysses*.

Gilbert's plan is reproduced on page xxiii of the introduction in the Penguin edition.

While they are interesting, I don't think we need to bother our heads about all these associations.

So I have provided a simplified plan, including all the original Homeric titles which are useful in navigating the book *and I recommend that you write them (in pencil)* at the head of each episode in your Penguin edition. I have given you a page reference for each episode, and numerous text references to the Penguin edition in the text.

Penguin/Vintage have since published a new edition which I do not recommend. It has very small print, which I find difficult to read, and my page references will not fit!

Happy Odyssey!

ULYSSES: THE EPISODES

Episode 1: TELEMACHUS The Tower 8a.m.... 2

Episode 2: NESTOR The School 10a.m.............. 8

Episode 3: PROTEUS The Strand 11a.m. 11

Episode 4: CALYPSO The House 8a.m........... 17

Episode 5: LOTUS-EATERS The Bath 10a.m. 22

Episode 6: HADES The Graveyard 11a.m. 26

Episode 7: AEOLUS The Newspaper 12 noon 33

Episode 8: LESTRYGONIANS The Lunch 1p.m. 40

Episode 9: SCYLLA AND CHARYBDIS The Library 2p.m. 45

Episode 10: WANDERING ROCKS The Streets 3p.m. 51

Episode 11: SIRENS The Concert Room 4p.m. 60

Episode 12: CYCLOPS The Tavern 5p.m........ 66

Episode 13: NAUSICAA The Rocks 6p.m. 75

Episode 14: OXEN OF THE SUN The Hospital 10p.m. 82

Episode 15: CIRCE The Brothel 12 midnight.. 95

Episode 16: EUMAEUS The Shelter 1a.m..... 113

Episode 17: ITHACA Part 1 The House 2a.m. 121

Episode 17A: ITHACA, part two 127
Episode 18: PENELOPE The Bed 135

PART I

ULYSSES BY JAMES JOYCE

Notes on Episode 1: TELEMACHUS (pages 1-28).

All page numbers refer to the Penguin edition, NOT the Vintage edition of 2022.

Joyce named this episode 'Telemachus' after the first episode in Homer's Odyssey. Telemachus was the son of Odysseus (aka Ulysses) who was searching for his father, absent for many years on his way back from the Trojan War. The parallel is that Stephen finds a (sort of) spiritual father in Mr Bloom, whom he will meet later on.

The date is 16 June 1904. The time is 8 a.m. The scene: the Martello Tower on the seashore at Sandycove, near Dublin. Martello Towers are small defensive forts, built around the coasts of Britain and Ireland during the Napoleonic wars, as a protection against invasion by the French. The one at Sandycove is now a Joyce Museum, well worth visiting. In this first episode, three young men are living in the tower. They are:

Malachi 'Buck' Mulligan, a clever medical student with a sarcastic wit. The character is based on Oliver St John Gogarty, a friend of Joyce, who became a well-known Dublin surgeon and writer.

Stephen Dedalus, an aspiring writer, very self-absorbed and tormented. Stephen is largely based on Joyce's younger self. His childhood and student years are described in the earlier novel, *A Portrait of the Artist as a Young Man* (1916).

and

Haines, an upper class English student who admires Stephen's intellectual brilliance. He is interested in Irish culture and literature but tends to see Ireland as an English colony.

The opening sentence: *Stately, plump Buck Mulligan came from the stairhead, bearing a bowl of lather on which a mirror and a razor lay crossed* (to resemble a crucifix). He is reciting a parody version of the Catholic Mass.

Mulligan has come up to the open-air top of the tower to have a shave. He calls for his friend, Stephen Dedalus, to come up and join him. His nickname for Stephen is 'Kinch' meaning a knife-blade. Mulligan loves to make fun of Stephen, telling him his Greek surname is absurd and calling him a 'jesuit', although both of them are lapsed Catholics.

Stephen complains about Haines, the Englishman, and asks how long he will be staying. (p 2). During the night, Haines was having a nightmare and *raving all night about a black panther.* (p 3)

P 3 line 7 from the end: *God, he said quietly. Isn't the sea what Algy calls it: a grey sweet mother?*
'Algy' is the Victorian poet Algernon Charles Swinburne. *Thalatta* is Greek for the sea. From the sea as mother, we move quickly to Stephen's mother:

P 4 *The aunt thinks you killed your mother*...Mulligan reproaches Stephen because, when his dying mother asked him to kneel and pray for her, he refused.

Stephen remembers, painfully, his mother's death and the dream he had about her: *silently, in a dream, she had come to him after her death*...This passage will recur several times in later chapters.

And yet, as Mulligan mockingly observes, he insists on wearing mourning clothes. *He kills his mother but he can't wear grey trousers.* (p 5).

P 5-6 Mulligan shows Stephen his face in the mirror and refers to a line of Oscar Wilde's about Caliban, also seeing his face in a mirror. Stephen says: *It is a symbol of Irish art. The cracked looking glass of a servant.* Mulligan is impressed by Stephen's cleverness.

P 6 bottom line: *Young shouts of moneyed voices.* This obscure passage seems to be Stephen's recollection of the 'ragging' of a fellow student. Just read it and move on! Until Stephen says *Let him* (Haynes) *stay*. But Mulligan (not entirely insensitive) wants to know why Stephen is upset.

P 8 Stephen tells Mulligan that he was offended by a remark Mulligan made to his Aunt about Stephen. *('O it's only Dedalus whose mother is beastly dead.')* Stephen regards this as an offence, not to his mother but to himself. But he continues to brood about his dead mother and to relive the ghoulish dream in which her ghost appeared to him.

P 9 Mulligan tells him that he is an impossible person and that he should *give up the moody brooding*. He quotes some lines from a song by the Irish poet W B Yeats (*And no more turn aside and brood)*. Stephen relates that he sang this song to his mother (from the next room) when she was dying. *In a dream, silently, she had come to him...* (p 10).

P 11 *Liliata rutilantium*... part of a Latin prayer for the dying. See also note on p 27.

Mulligan tells Stephen that the Englishman, Haines, admires him and that he should '*touch him for a quid.*' He and Stephen are both hard up. The three men have breakfast downstairs in the tower's living room. (pp 12-13) The milk woman has not yet arrived, but Haines sees her approaching the tower.

Haines tells Mulligan he makes strong tea and Mulligan replies (p13):
 '*When I makes tea, I makes tea, as old Mother Grogan said. And when I makes water I makes water.*' (*Begob, ma'am*, says Mrs Cahill, *God send you don't make them in the one pot.*)

P 15 The old woman arrives to deliver the milk. Haines tries to speak to her in Irish (Gaelic)but she thinks he is talking French! As well as being herself, she represents the spirit of ancient Ireland, sometimes called: *the poor old woman.* The conversation involving her continues till p 17.

P 18 Haines says he would like to make a collection of Stephen's sayings. Stephen says: *Would I make money out of it?*
 Stephen and Mulligan discuss their shortage of cash.

Mulligan continues his teasing mockery as they prepare to go out. He tells Haines that Stephen has a theory about *Hamlet* in which *he proves by algebra that Hamlet's grandson is Shakespeare's grandfather and that he himself is the ghost of his own father* (p 21).

P 22 Mulligan declaims a verse that makes fun of Christian doctrine (*I'm the queerest young fellow that ever you heard*) and a discussion about religious belief follows. Haines tells Stephen he should be able to escape from the influence of his Catholic upbringing. Stephen tells him that he is the servant of two masters, one English and one Italian (meaning the Pope).

P 24-25 *The proud potent titles…* In this rather obscure passage, Stephen is thinking about Christian doctrines (learned at his Jesuit school) and the triumphant way in which the church dismisses heretics *(A herd of heresies fleeing with mitres awry.)* Perhaps he sees Mulligan as the devil tempting him as he tempted Christ. They go down to the beach where Mulligan has a swim while Haines minds his clothes.

Stephen arranges to meet them later at a pub (The Ship) at 12.30. It will be an appointment that he does not keep.

P 27.*Liliata rutilantium…*is part of a prayer that was recited at Stephen's mother's death bed. It translates as 'May the troop of confessors, glowing like lilies, surround you. May the choir of virgins, jubilant, take you in.'

Note the twice occurring phrase *agenbite of inwit* which Stephen says to himself. It was the title of a 14th century devotional book and it means 'the gnawing of conscience'. (pp 15 and 16)

It has just occurred to me that there are a lot of mothers in this chapter.

Notes on Episode 2: NESTOR (28-45)

(From now on page numbers will be indicated just as numbers.)

Place: The School. Time: 10 a.m.
In Homer's Odyssey, Telemachus seeks news of his lost father (Odysseus), from King Nestor who was one of Odysseus's comrades in the war with Troy. In Joyce's version, the powerful older man is ironically represented by Mr Deasy, the mean and bigoted headmaster at the school where Stephen is employed as a teacher.

As the episode begins, we find Stephen teaching Roman history to a class of boys. It's a bit like any schoolteacher story except that we have access to his private thoughts through the 'stream of consciousness'. Stephen asks the boys what they know about the Roman general Pyrrhus. Armstrong, a rather hapless boy, says the word means 'a pier' and Stephen tells them that a pier is *a disappointed bridge*, a witticism which pleases him but is lost on his pupils.

Stephen switches suddenly to literature (*Tell us a story, sir*) and asks a boy called Talbot to read from Milton's *Lycidas*. As he listens, Stephen's mind wanders to recollections of his studies of Aristotle in a university library in Paris. The phrase *Through the dear might of Him that walked the waves* (31) reminds him of Jesus and his enigmatic response about the tribute money. This prompts him to offer the boys a riddle to solve: *The cock crew...* (32).

They haven't a clue and quickly give up. But the solution is equally puzzling:

The fox burying his grandmother under a holly bush.

I have been unable to find out the origin of this line which sounds like a proverb or a fragment from an Aesop fable. But we know that Stephen has recently buried his mother and that her deathbed reproaches still bother him. (See later, 33, mid-page) *His mother's prostrate body…*)

The boys rush off to play hockey, leaving behind only Cyril Sargent, a rather pathetic boy who needs to show Stephen his maths.

34 Stephen is kind and gentle with Sargent; he seems ugly and futile: *Yet someone had loved him, borne him in her arms and in her heart*. This reflection leads him back once again to thoughts of his own mother. Stephen, looking at Sargent thinks: *Like him was I, these sloping shoulders, this gracelessness* (34, mid-page).

35 Later, Stephen collects his wages (three pounds, twelve shillings) from Mr Deasy, the headmaster. After handing over the money, Mr Deasy gives Stephen a lecture on thrift and frugality (36). Mr Deasy is an Ulster protestant with fierce loyalties to England. He tells Stephen that an Englishman is always proud to say *I paid my way* and owes nobody anything. Stephen mentally lists all his debtors with the amounts outstanding.

38 Now Mr Deasy switches to claiming rebel (i.e. Irish) blood too, on his mother's side. He is really quite obnoxious, but there is worse to come. He types out a

letter (composed entirely of clichés), about foot and mouth disease in cattle and asks Stephen to use his contacts to get it printed in the papers. Finally he starts an antisemitic rant about England being doomed because it is *in the hands of the jews* (41).

The harlot's cry from street to street
Shall weave old England's winding sheet

This couplet is from a poem by William Blake.

Stephen demonstrates his disagreement and shows in his thoughts that he has sympathy with the Jewish people and their plight. This is important for us to note because we know that the other male protagonist of *Ulysses*, soon to be introduced, is the Jewish Mr Bloom.

After a parting witticism from Mr Deasy about Ireland and the 'jews', Stephen, with an ironic thought about his boss's 'wisdom', leaves the school, never to return.

NB: there are two much-quoted epigrams from Stephen in this chapter, both on p 42:

History… is a nightmare from which I am trying to awake (meaning the Irish history of oppression) and

(God is) *A shout in the street.* Joyce was very scared by thunderstorms and had the idea that God was shouting at him!

Notes on Episode 3: PROTEUS (45-64)

Time:11.a.m. Place: The Strand (beach).

Stephen walks along the beach at Sandymount Strand.

Proteus was a sea-god in Greek mythology who was slippery, always changing his shape to evade questioning. In Homer, he is held down firmly by Menelaus who is then able to extract information from him about the fate of Odysseus and his men. The episode in Ulysses consists entirely of Stephen's thoughts, his stream of consciousness. His thought processes are like Proteus: the shape and content constantly changing.

This is a difficult chapter. But be not afraid! You won't understand much of it at a first reading, but you can enjoy the poetic language and, with a few signposts from me, you can catch the drift of Stephen's thoughts and feelings. Stephen is in a much more cheerful mood now; observing everything as he strolls across the sands, rehearsing his poetic skills. **I do not recommend** that you try to track down the meaning of all the references to philosophy and literature in the episode. I think it's much better just to accompany Stephen on his walk, admire his intellectual depth and breadth, catch an allusion here and there but avoid trying to engage him in argument. However, if you really want to look up a phrase that is bothering you, I recommend the website called The Joyce Project. Sub-section: *Ulysses.*

The first line: *Ineluctable mode of the visible*. The word 'ineluctable' means unavoidable or inescapable and Stephen is noting that our first and lasting impressions of things come through our eyes. Then he thinks about the other senses: he shuts his eyes, listens and hears the crackling of his boots walking over the shells and the sand.

I will just explain those two German words in italics. *Nacheinander* means 'one after another' and *Nebeinander* means 'together with'. They were used by a German aesthetic philosopher to indicate the difference between poetry (progressive) and painting (static). You really don't need to bother with this!

Soon (46) Stephen spots two midwives, one carrying her professional bag, which leads Stephen to imagine that it contains a misbirth (miscarriage) with a trailing navel cord: this in turn gives rise to a humorous fantasy of navel cords all twining back like telephone cables to the Garden of Eden. In the last paragraph he thinks about his own birth.

Suddenly, real life intervenes in his thoughts (47, line 13). He mustn't forget to deliver Mr Deasy's letter. And he had intended to call at his Aunt Sara's. She is Stephen's father's sister, the wife of his paternal uncle, Richie Goulding, a legal clerk. Walter, Stephen's cousin, is their son. Now we seem to be at the Goulding's house: *I pull the wheezy bell of their shuttered cottage* (bottom of 47). We stay with the Gouldings for a while but Stephen is distracted by memories of his Jesuit schooldays (49) and bitter ruminations about the church and the clergy: wondering why he ever wanted to become a priest. He goes on to reproach himself for wasting his time over scholarly ambitions as a student in Paris.

Waking again from his reveries, he again becomes aware of the beach (and its debris) –

and realises that he has gone past the way to Aunt Sara's (bottom of 50). The visit turns out to have been an imagined one and we realise that Joyce has played a neat little narrative trick on us.

Mixed up memories of Paris follow and Stephen mocks his own naïve ambitions (*You were going to do wonders, what?* (p 52, para 2). Paris was ended by that telegram: *Mother dying come home father. The aunt thinks you killed your mother. (*See Episode 1*).*

54 He gives us more memories of Paris and in particular his meetings with Kevin Egan (real name: Joseph Casey), once an Irish revolutionary, now a refugee. The language is vivid and full of striking images; a mixture of the poetic and the everyday. Stephen appears to be practicing his facility with words, rather like the young Joyce.

55 Stephen has come to the edge of the sea. He turns towards the south shore and thinks about the Martello tower which is now visible. *The cold domed room of the tower waits.* But he will not sleep there tonight.

Last para: He sees a dead dog and a wrecked boat. Then (56) a live dog, with two human owners in the distance. He thinks of the invaders who have historically landed here: Vikings and whalers. He was afraid of the dog, until it ran back to its owners and he feels ashamed.

57 *He saved men from drowning and you shake at a cur's yelping*, he tells himself. 'He' is Mulligan who is known to have rescued several people from the sea. Stephen wonders if he would jump in if put to the test?

A woman and a man. I see her skirties. He watches the two people with the dog (a man and a woman). They are gypsy cockle pickers, but he imagines them as exotic, romantic figures, perhaps even vampires.

59 *Shouldering their bags, they trudged on, the red Egyptians.* Egyptians here means travellers or gypsies. *White thy fambles, red thy gan...* He is quoting a verse in a gypsy language (known as 'cant'). It means: 'White thy cheeks and red thy mouth'.

60 Pleased with some poetic lines he has thought up. *He comes, pale vampire, his batsails bloodying the sea, mouth to her mouth's kiss.*

Happy with these phrases, he feels he must quickly note them down (*Put a pin in that chap, will you?*) He tears a piece of blank paper off the end of Mr Deasy's letter and scribbles the words down, using a rock as a table.

Later (p 61) he is thinks longingly about an idealised woman (*She trusts me, her hand gentle, the long lashed eyes.*) She is a real girl he has seen in Dublin; but he remembers her *curse of God stays, suspenders and yellow stockings* and is disillusioned. He lies down for a while, still observing everything and putting it into words.

62 He passes urine and describes extravagantly the water he has created as it flows from him onto the sand. His thoughts turn to drowned corpses, one of which is expected to surface soon in the bay. Their dissolution is brilliantly and hideously described.

63 But now it's time to leave the Strand. He worries about his teeth. He picks his nose. And looks for his handkerchief, which he lent to Mulligan in the first episode.

Remember? *Lend us a loan of your nose rag to wipe my razor.* Unable to find a handkerchief, he lays the snot carefully on a rock; looks behind to see if anyone has seen him; sees a three master, *silently moving, a silent ship.*

*

And that is the end of the first section, or prelude, of *Ulysses*. In the episode that follows, we meet Leopold Bloom, Joyce's version of Odysseus: very different from the original but also with some points of similarity. Stephen's story is also continued as their paths cross around Dublin and finally – they meet.

Reading gets much, much easier (for a while), so if you can't wait any longer to meet Leopold Bloom in the next episode (Calypso) – just go for it!

PART II

Notes on Episode 4: CALYPSO (65-85)

The time: 8 a.m. (again). The place: The House.

Joyce named this episode 'Calypso', after the nymph in Homer's Odyssey who detains Ulysses for seven years on her island love-nest.

Joyce's version of Odysseus is not a soldier hero, but a mild-mannered 38-year-old man, generally regarded by his fellow Dubliners as Jewish although his mother was a gentile, so he is really only half Jewish. He has also been baptised three times and enjoys having a pork kidney for breakfast. However he has absorbed some knowledge of Judaism from his father.

In this chapter, we are privileged to sit in Mr Bloom's head, sharing his thoughts and feelings, and his reactions as he walks round Dublin on the 16th of June 1904. Joyce enables us to do this by using his technique of 'stream of consciousness'. We shall find that Bloom is a keen and curious observer of human life, with a great capacity for empathy with his fellow men, women and even animals. Incidentally, this was the date on which James Joyce and his wife-to-be, Nora Barnacle, first 'walked out' together.

First sentence:
Mr Leopold Bloom ate with relish the inner organs of beasts and fowls.

We meet Mr Bloom in his kitchen, at No. 7 Eccles Street, where he is thinking of preparing a tray to take up to his wife (Molly) and also about going round to the butcher's for a tasty kidney. He has a conversation with the cat, who mews: *Mkgano!* (later amplified). Note the beautiful descriptions of the cat. He calls up the stairs to Molly, (who says she wants only a cup of tea), to tell her he is going round the corner. Her reply is *Mn.*

Out in the street, it's a warm summer morning. Passing Larry O'Rourke's pub (69) he says good day to Larry. He wonders how pub landlords make their money; by the way, a 'curate' is Dubliners' name for an assistant barman.

Reaching Dlugacz's butcher's shop (70) he waits to be served. In front of him is next-door's maid, a sturdy young woman whom he rather fancies. It would have been nice to walk behind her, admiring her 'hams', but she moves off too quickly.

The kidney costs three pence (today's 1p coin equals 2.4 old pennies)

On his way back to the house (72) he ruminates about an advertisement on the butcher's newspaper wrapping, offering opportunities to invest in a farm in Palestine. It sounds attractive but in the end, '*Nothing doing,*' he decides. For the reader, this is some early evidence of his Jewish ancestry. And possibly that of the pork-butcher.

Citron and Mastiansky are old Jewish friends whom Bloom doesn't seem to have seen lately.

As a cloud begins to cover the sun (73) the image of Mediterranean brightness fades and is replaced by gloomy visions of grey, barren landscapes, old age and death. Arriving back home (75) he is cheered by the thought of breakfast and being near Molly's *ample, bedwarmed flesh.* Back in the kitchen, he puts the kettle on.

74. The postman has brought two letters and a card. One letter is from their 15-year-old daughter, Milly, but the other is addressed to 'Mrs Marion Bloom' in *a bold hand.*
And his quick heart slowed at once.
Bloom suspects, rightly, that this letter is from Hugh 'Blazes' Boylan, Molly's concert promoter (she is a talented soprano). Boylan's letter will be confirming his appointment for a sexual encounter at 4 o'clock. We are not actually given this information, because Joyce likes to conceal vital details of the plot, giving only the slightest of clues, which we have to put together as we go along. It can be fun to discover the clues, but for a first reading it really does help to have a few tips about what's going on.

Thoughts of what will happen in the bedroom at 4 o'clock continue to haunt and torture Mr Bloom throughout the day, but he decides to keep out of her way, avoid a confrontation and not say anything to Molly about her infidelity.

When he takes her tray up (76) he *sees a strip of torn-open envelope* peeping out from under her pillow – and asks who the letter is from. She tells him that Boylan is coming round with the concert programme.

Leopold asks her what she will be singing: she tells him 'La Ci Darem' and 'Love's Old Sweet Song'. 'La ci darem in mano' (Put your hand in mine) is a seduction aria from Mozart's opera *Don Giovanni*; a scene which she and Boylan will be re-enacting in her bedroom later in the day. 'Love's Old Sweet Song' was a very popular Victorian song whose plaintive melody haunts the whole book.

Ulysses is full of songs and to hear them in your head adds greatly to the pleasure of reading.

Changing the subject, Molly asks her husband to explain a word she has come across in the lurid romance she is reading. The word is 'metempsychosis' which the knowledgeable, self-taught Bloom tells her, is a Greek word meaning 'transmigration of souls'. He tries to explain the concept, but Molly is not very interested. She asks him to get her another book by Paul de Kock ('*Nice name he has*').

A smell of burning (79) reminds Bloom that he has left the kidney in the frying pan, and he dashes down, just in time to save it. Over an enjoyable breakfast he reads the letter from their daughter, Milly, who is away in Mullingar (a small inland town, not far from Dublin), where she is working for a photographer. He thinks (80) about the day she was born and Mrs Thornton, the midwife, who was later to tell him that '*poor little Rudy wouldn't live.*' This brief clue tells us that, after Milly, the Blooms had a baby boy who died in infancy. Later on, we will learn that he sadly lived only 11 days and is still in both his parents' thoughts. Ever since Rudy died, nearly 11 years ago, their sex life has been 'incomplete'.

81 *All dimpled cheeks and curls, Your head it simply swirls.* These fragments of verse are from a popular

song of the day called: 'Seaside Girls'. (Find it on YouTube).

Bloom notes that Milly is growing up now and has attracted the attention of a young man in Mullingar: ready for *young kisses: the first*.

Will happen, yes. Prevent. Useless: can't move. He remembers his first kiss with Molly. He is also thinking about how he can't prevent Molly having sex with Boylan.

82 After finishing his breakfast, Mr Bloom lets the cat out, and goes to the outdoor privy ('the jakes'), to open his bowels. While he waits, he reads a magazine article about a man who has won a prize for a short story. Perhaps he could write one too. Then his thoughts turn again to Molly and he remembers the evening when they first met Boylan; and Molly danced with him. Finally (85) he hears the church bells chiming and he says '*Poor Dignam!*' He has remembered that he has to go to the funeral of a friend called Patrick Dignam at 11 a.m. (The funeral is the subject of episode 6, known as 'Hades'.)

Note: P 81 *Those lovely seaside girls* This is a mildly suggestive music hall song sung by Blazes Boylan, according to Milly and also by his nephew, young Bannion.

Notes on Episode 5: LOTUS-EATERS (85-107)

The time: 10 a.m. The place: streets of Dublin.

Joyce called this chapter 'Lotus-eaters', after the episode in The Odyssey, in which Odysseus's men are given the Lotus plant to eat. This induces a dreamy, lethargic state of inertia: perhaps similar to the effects of cannabis.
  By lorries along Sir John Rogerson's Quay…

This episode follows straight on from 'Calypso'.

Mr Bloom is now walking alongside the river Liffey, looking at the shops and at some poor children playing. Passing a tea merchant in Westland Row, he muses about tea-growing and the sleepiness and lethargy he imagines to be the effect of hot Eastern climates. Remnants of physics float through his mind too.

At the post office (87) he collects a letter addressed to him under his assumed name of 'Henry Flower'. (Flower = Bloom). In the street again, he is anxious to read the letter but is waylaid by the annoying Mr McCoy (89-90). McCoy asks about the forthcoming funeral of Paddy Dignam. He keeps on and on about Dignam's surprisingly sudden death. While he pretends to listen, Bloom is trying to catch sight of the alluring silk-stocking-clad ankles of a haughty-looking, upper-class woman emerging from a hotel and about to get into a cab. His view is interrupted, first by McCoy, and then by a passing tram.

91 He glances at his newspaper (*The Freeman's Journal*) and reads an advertisement for 'Plumtree's Potted Meat'.

> What is home without
> Plumtree's Potted Meat?
> Incomplete.
> With it an abode of bliss.

This little slogan will recur to his mind at intervals during the day. Its sexual connotations will be revealed later, (in case not already obvious!). Bloom and McCoy talk about their wives going on singing tours. McCoy, a devious character, is probably lying about his wife who has not got much of a voice. During the conversation, a line from *Love's Old Sweet Song* drifts through Bloom's mind. This is one of Molly's favourites and will feature in her concert tour. (We should listen to it!) He finally gets rid of McCoy and continues on his leisurely stroll.

93 A playbill reminds him of Ophelia's suicide in *Hamlet* and that in turn reminds him of his father, who also took his own life. Sadly, he remembers some of his father's words.

Then he passes some horses and feels empathy with them.

94 He hums a couple of lines in Italian: *La ci darem la mano*. This is an aria from Mozart's opera *Don Giovanni* ('Put your hand in mine'), which Molly will also sing on her concert tour. The aria is sung by the lecherous Don who is trying to seduce a peasant girl on her wedding day. Bloom knows that 'Blazes' Boylan

(the concert promoter), has a date to seduce the willing Molly at 4 o'clock. He is unhappily reminded of this many times during the day. You can find *La ci darem* on YouTube: the version with Bryn Terfel and Hei-Kyung Hong from the Metropolitan Opera, in my opinion, is the best.

However, Leopold has his own fantasy about an adulterous relationship. At last (94) he has a chance to open his letter which is a reply from a woman calling herself 'Martha', with whom he has started a clandestine correspondence. They have never met in person so this is similar to an internet romance. The letter is saucy but also rather pathetic.

Do tell me what kind of perfume does your wife use. I want to know.

After reading and reacting to the letter he enters All Hallows Church (p 97) and watches the service. He notes that religion and Communion seems to make people feel better; he is not a believer, but he appreciates devotional music; he has some rather sceptical thoughts about Confession.

Leaving the church (103) he walks south along Westland Row and calls at the chemist to order a repeat of some special skin lotion for Molly. For himself, he buys a cake of lemon-scented soap. You can still buy one of these if you visit the old Sweny's Pharmacy in Dublin. As Bloom observes, '*Chemists rarely move.*' (But this one has turned into a sort of James Joyce memorial gift shop.)

Next (105) he meets a character called 'Bantam' Lyons who talks about the Gold Cup race at Ascot, to be run later in the day. He wants to look at Bloom's newspaper to check on the runners. Bloom says, '*You can keep it. I was just going to throw it away.*' Lyons thinks this is a coded tip for a horse called 'Throwaway' and goes off excitedly, intending to put some money on this 20 – 1 outsider.

(Records show that a horse called 'Throwaway' actually did win the Ascot Gold Cup on 16 June 1904 at 20 – 1!)

Finally, Bloom heads for the Turkish bath, looking forward, in a wonderful paragraph, to a luxuriating wallow in warm lemon-scented soapy water.

Notes on Episode 6: HADES (107-147)

This episode takes place on the way to the funeral of Paddy Dignam, and at the graveyard (Prospect Cemetery, Glasnevin), for the funeral itself. The name 'Hades' refers to the visit made by Odysseus to the land of the Dead.

Time: 11.a.m.

First line: *Martin Cunningham, first, poked his silk-hatted head into the creaking carriage and, entering deftly, seated himself.*

Four men will travel in a horse-drawn carriage across the city of Dublin, from Paddy Dignam's home in Sandymount, on the South East side, to the Prospect Cemetery, Glasnevin, in the North West, where he will be buried. They are:

- Martin Cunningham, a decent, liberal-minded man
- Simon Dedalus, father of Stephen Dedalus, the young man whom we met in episode one
- Jack Power (polite and courteous)
- Leopold Bloom, the outsider, desperate to be accepted

For most of this episode we are hearing Bloom's private thoughts. Speech is indicated, as in the foregoing chapters, by a dash.

108 Bloom sees an old woman peeping out of a window. He muses on the attraction funerals seem to

have for women and their role in deathbed rituals. (*Glad to see us go we give them such trouble coming.*)

109 When the carriage moves off, Bloom spots Stephen Dedalus in the street and points him out to his father, Simon. Dedalus senior has a rant about his son's association with the disreputable medical student, Malachi 'Buck' Mulligan (see episode one). *The Goulding faction*, mentioned disdainfully by Simon are the family of his wife's brother, the impoverished lawyer's clerk, Richie Goulding.

110 Bloom thinks about fathers and sons. If only the infant, Rudy, had lived, he would have had a son too. He recalls the day when Molly's aroused sexual appetite led to Rudy's conception (*Give us a touch, Poldy. God, I'm dying for it. How life begins.)*

111 The men discover traces of food on the leather seats. Or something worse?
    Note that 'Corny' is Corny Kelleher, the funeral director.

112 The carriage stops by the gas works and the Dogs' home. Bloom remembers his father's old dog, Athos. His father, in his dying note, had asked Leopold to take care of the dog. *Be good to Athos, Leopold, is my last wish.*
    They feel a few spots of rain and Mr Dedalus remarks that the sky is *as uncertain as a child's bottom.*

Note: 'The hazard' is a cab stand and 'jarvies' are cab-drivers. All the cabs are horse-drawn.

114 *I tore up the envelope?* Bloom is trying to remember what he did with the envelope from Martha Clifford's letter (previous episode, 5). They pass the Antient Concert Rooms, perhaps reminding him of Molly, who has performed there. He wonders about going to a theatre in the evening. Note Bloom's thought: *he's coming in the afternoon. Her songs.* (7th line from bottom). He means Blazes Boylan, Molly's lover is coming, ostensibly to discuss the songs in her concert programme. Then they all see Boylan himself, standing in the street and doffing his straw hat.

115 *Just that moment I was thinking.* Is Bloom's comment to himself. And *Worst man in Dublin.* He wonders what Molly sees in the raffish impresario with whom she will have sex that afternoon.

116 Mr Power asks Bloom about Molly's concert tour, referring to her has 'Madame' in a respectful tone.

Voglio e non vorrei. No. *vorrei e non.Mi trema un poco il.* ('I want to and I don't want to. I am trembling a little.') More snatches of the duet between the Don and Zerlina from *Don Giovanni.* Bloom is thinking about Molly as the seduced wife, a role she is about to play in her bedroom as well as on the concert platform.

117 *They passed under the huge cloaked Liberator's form* (the statue of Daniel O'Connell on the North end of O'Connell Bridge over the Liffey). O'Connell was a Catholic lawyer who successfully campaigned for Catholic emancipation in the nineteenth century and later became a member of parliament.

Of the tribe of Reuben. They pass a well-known Jewish moneylender (*a tall blackbearded figure*). This is embarrassing for Bloom as a fellow-Jew. He tries to avoid the association by starting to tell a joke about Reuben and his son which is *going the rounds.*

119 They discuss Paddy Dignam's possible cause of death. *(He went very suddenly.)*
   White horses appear, drawing a hearse with a child's coffin. Bloom is reminded again of the death of baby Rudy.

120 Mr Power starts talking about suicide being a great disgrace to the family. More embarrassment for Bloom, whose father killed himself by drinking poison. Power doesn't know this, but considerate Martin Cunningham does, and he tries to deflect the topic. Bloom remembers that Martin has an alcoholic wife who makes his home life miserable.

121 Bloom thinks about the inquest on his father's death. The carriage speeds up. They pass Eccles Street where the Blooms live.

122 They are held up by a drove of cattle and sheep on their way to their death (at the slaughterhouse). Bloom suggests there should be a special tramway for funerals. Once, the others say, a hearse capsized and upset the coffin on the road. Bloom has fantasies about hearses capsizing and the corpse falling out of the coffin. What happens to a body after death?

124 They cross the Royal canal and Bloom thinks about travelling to visit his daughter Milly in Mullingar: perhaps by water via the canal.

125 The journey continues. They pass a house which was the scene of the notorious Childs murder, which resulted in a celebrated trial that ended with the defendant's acquittal.

126 They arrive at the cemetery and the coffin is unloaded from the hearse. They mingle with other mourners. They are all men: it was the custom in Ireland that only men went to the burial.

127 Martin Cunningham whispers to Mr Power about Bloom's father's suicide in the Queen's Hotel, Ennis. They talk about Dignam's family and how many children he has left fatherless. Ned Lambert greets Simon Dedalus. They go into the chapel (129).

The funeral service takes place, to the accompaniment of Bloom's thoughts.

132 Leaving the chapel, they pass Daniel O'Connell's grave and monument. Mr Dedalus points out his wife's grave .He is quite upset and says: *I'll soon be stretched beside her. Let Him take me when he likes.*

133 Bloom continues to brood on death and has sceptical thoughts about the Resurrection.

134 John Henry Menton (a disagreeable solicitor) asks *who is that chap behind with Tom Kernan?* Ned Lambert tells him it is Bloom who is married *to*

Madam Marion Tweedy that was, is. I mean the soprano. She's his wife.

Menton remembers Molly: *She was a fine-looking woman.* Looking at Bloom,

In God's name, he says, *What did she marry a coon like that for? She had plenty of game in her, then.*

(Contempt for Bloom as a Jew and an outsider is widespread. Although Cunningham, Power and Dedalus are more friendly and less prejudiced.)

134-5 John O'Connell, the caretaker of the cemetery appears. Simon Dedalus dolefully says *I am come to pay you another visit.* John O'Connell tries to cheer them up with a funny story about two drunks looking for the grave of a friend.

136 Bloom wonders what it's like for the caretaker to have his home in the graveyard. What would his wife think about it?

Bloom thinks about sex in graveyards and his mind wanders again to the decay and dissolution of corpses. He thinks about dying and what the moments before death must feel like. Suppose you were buried alive?

138 The burial is completed by the gravediggers.

141 Hynes, the reporter, takes the names of the mourners, 12 in all, plus a mysterious man in a macintosh, whom no-one seems to know. Hynes writes his name down as M'Intosh. He is referred to in future episodes as 'Mr M'Intosh'.

142 (bottom of page) Hynes says *Let us go round by the chief's grave.* 'The chief' is Charles Stewart

Parnell (1846-91), the revered Irish republican political leader, who fell from grace as a result of his affair with a married woman (Kittie O'Shea). After his death it was widely hoped that he might somehow return.

143 Bloom walks among the gravestones, reading the inscriptions, his thoughts ironical, yet fearful.

145 He sees a rat at the bottom of a stone crypt.

146-7 The episode ends in an uncomfortable confrontation with the standoffish Menton. Bloom kindly points out a dent in Menton's hat. Menton stares at him and then says a curt *thankyou.*

And Bloom thinks: *Thank you. How grand we are this morning!*

Notes on Episode 7: AEOLUS (147-189)

Time: 12 noon. Place: The newspaper office

In The Odyssey, Aeolus is the god of the winds who gives Odysseus a bag containing all the winds, including the dangerous ones: unfortunately his sailors open the bag and they are blown disastrously off course.

Everyone in this episode is 'long-winded' except Bloom. Although a lot of the narration is carried by his unspoken 'stream of consciousness'.

You will notice that the chapter is divided into short sections each headed by

A NEWSPAPER HEADLINE IN CAPITAL LETTERS.
(followed here by the page number in parentheses).

We start with an impression of the Dublin trams manoeuvring in front of Nelson's Pillar ((Dublin's version of Nelson's column, which stood outside the main Post Office until it was blown up by Irish republicans in 1966).

We are on our way to the shared offices of a number of Dublin newspapers including *The Freeman's Journal* and *The Evening Telegraph*. Mr Bloom is there on business because he needs to get an old advertisement renewed, on behalf of a client. That's his job, an 'advertising canvasser' who places advertisements in the papers for commission. Creating the ad and getting it published for his client requires a number of difficult steps. First, he needs to get a copy of the merchant's previous advertisement to which he wants to add a crossed keys motif. (His client is a tea, wine and spirits merchant called Alexander *Keyes*.) Red Murray obligingly cuts it out for him. Then he has to take it to Mr Nannetti the foreman of the *Telegraph* to ask him to publish the new advert. But Nannetti insists that Mr Keyes must pay for a three month renewal. So Bloom has to find Keyes and get his agreement.

Of course if he wants a par (7 lines from bottom of 148). 'A par' is a paragraph, meaning a piece of text.

Bloom's pursuit of this deal and his scurrying in and out of the newspaper offices form a thread running through the episode.

WILLIAM BRAYDEN, ESQUIRE OF OAKLANDS, SANDYMOUNT. (148)

The owner of the Press makes a solemn entrance. Red Murray thinks he looks like Jesus; Bloom thinks he's more like Mario, the tenor. Bloom makes his way through to the print room.

HOW A GREAT DAILY ORGAN IS TURNED OUT (150)
He finds Mr Nannetti, the foreman and thinks about his Italian origin. The clanking and thumping of the presses is now a noisy background.

152 Bloom shows the cutting of the old advertisement to Mr Nannetti and explains (above the racket), the change he wants made.

154 Note that the printed papers are now falling out of the machine and saying *Sllt. Sllt.*

AND IT WAS THE FEAST OF THE PASSOVER (155)

Bloom watches a typesetter and admires his ability to read the words backwards. It reminds him of his father reading, from right to left, the Pessach (Passover) story in the Hebrew Passover service book, Hagadah. He tries to recollect the words of one of the Hagadah songs and gets it a bit mixed up:*and then the lamb and the cat*...Bloom goes down the stairs to the editor's office where he hopes to be able to use the phone.

ERIN GREEN GEM OF THE SILVER SEA (156)

Meanwhile, in the office of Myles Crawford, the Editor and a number of Dublin worthies are gathering. Some are there on business; others seem to be idly passing the time of day.

We are introduced firstly to Professor MacHugh, who satirically murmurs *'The ghost walks'* as Bloom sidles in, aware, as always, of being an outsider and the butt of jokes.

Also present are Simon Dedalus (Stephen's father, whom we met at the funeral), and Ned Lambert. Ned is jeeringly reading aloud from the paper a highfalutin patriotic speech made by Dan Dawson (a well-known baker). Bloom tries to join in the intellectual conversation but is treated with coolness, as usual. J J O'Molloy, a failed barrister, comes in abruptly pushing the door knob into Bloom's back.

SAD (158)

Bloom meditates on O'Molloy's deterioration: *Cleverest fellow at the junior bar he used to be. Decline poor chap.*

Ned Lambert goes on reading from the paper until he is interrupted by the sudden arrival of the Editor, Myles Crawford, with *his scarlet beaky face crested by a comb of feathery hair.* Crawford (who seems to be drunk), and MacHugh greet each other with mock insults. The conversation continues. After a while Mr Bloom slips out to Crawford's office after asking permission to use his phone.

SPOT THE WINNER (162)

Lenehan comes in. He is something of a layabout and a scrounger who fancies himself as a wit and indeed is sometimes very funny, when Joyce allows him. He offers a racing tip for the Ascot Gold Cup which is going to be held that day. A group of ragged newsboys is heard outside, eager to get hold of the sports edition. Mr Bloom is heard on the phone, trying to track down his client.

A COLLISION ENSUES (163)

Bloom comes back in and bumps into Lenehan. After apologising, Bloom announces that he is just running round to Bachelor's Walk to look for his client. Myles Crawford responds satirically: *Begone! The world is before you.* They all watch, in amusement, the newsboys following Bloom and imitating his walk. After EXIT BLOOM (164) he is absent apart from a brief reappearance near the end of the episode.

Crawford wants to go and join Dedalus and Lambert, who have slipped off to the pub but he is detained by further discussion, now about the ancient Romans and their obsession with water-closets and sewers (166-7)

Next, Mr O'Madden Burke comes in, escorting Stephen Dedalus, who has come to deliver the letter on foot and mouth disease entrusted to him by Mr Deasy, the Headmaster in episode two (NESTOR), '*Youth led by Experience visits Notoriety*'. (Stephen, led by Burke visits Miles Crawford, the editor.)

? ? ? (167)

Lenehan sets them a riddle: *What opera resembles a railway line?*

Stephen, hands over Mr Deasy's 'Foot and mouth' letter.

LOST CAUSES (169)

The talk continues, with lots of classical references and oratorical flourishes from the senior members. The professor compares the Greeks to the Irish; and the English (their colonial masters), to the Romans.

And Lenehan finally delivers the answer to his feeble riddle ('The Rose of Castile'). Myles Crawford reminisces about great journalists of the past.

YOU CAN DO IT (171)

The editor asks Stephen to write something for him.

THE GREAT GALLAGHER (172)

Gallagher was a journalist who reported the notorious Phoenix Park Murders in which a group of Republican terrorists known as 'The Invincibles' ambushed and stabbed to death two senior British Civil

Service officials. Apparently part of this was in code. There is further discussion about this incident.

A DISTANT VOICE (173)

It appears that the voice is that of Bloom on the telephone.

174-7 There is further discussion of the Phoenix Park incident and other matters of which I don't think we need to check all the references. I recommend that you read it just as an innocent listener, catching the occasional connection.

Later on (A MAN OF HIGH MORALE, 178), Professor MacHugh recalls a moving oratorical speech by John F Taylor in which he imagines an Egyptian high priest trying to persuade Moses to abandon the 'inferior' culture, religion and language of 'the jews' and to embrace the superior way of life of the Egyptians. If Moses had succumbed, the speaker declares, *he would never have brought the chosen people out of their house of bondage.* The parallel is with the Irish patriots' struggle to preserve the Irish language.

OMINOUS – FOR HIM! (181)

J J O'Molloy remarks that Moses *died without having entered the land of promise.* To which Lenehan adds that he died *with a great future behind him.*

182 Taking up Stephen's suggestion, the remaining company now decide to follow Ned Lambert and Dedalus senior who have gone off for a drink.On the way, Stephen tells them his 'Parable of the Plums'

(starting in the section headlined DEAR DIRTY DUBLIN. (183)

RETURN OF BLOOM (185)

As they are walking, Bloom suddenly reappears, breathlessly, *caught in a whirl of newsboys.* Mr Keyes will only offer a two week renewal, he tells the editor, who rudely replies *well you tell him he can kiss my arse* (K.M.A.) And then: K.M.R.I.A. Stephen resumes his long tale about the two elderly Dublin ladies, but when he finally gets to the punchline, the reaction of his listeners is disappointing. In a return to the scene of the opening paragraph (also in front of Nelson's Pillar) we find that the trams have all been brought to a standstill by an electrical short circuit.

The main theme of this episode seems to be frustration and disappointment. Bloom fails to seal the deal for his advertisement; J J O'Molloy, the once promising barrister is reduced to unsuccessfully trying to cadge a loan from Myles Crawford; Moses dies before he can enter the Promised Land; Stephen's old ladies having climbed Nelson's pillar find that gazing up at the *one handled adulterer* gives them a stiff neck, and they are too tired to look down.

Even the trams are unable to move. And, of course, when the windbag is prematurely ripped open, Odysseus and his men are unable to return to their home in Ithaca.

Notes on Episode 8: LESTRYGONIANS (190-234)

In Homer's Odyssey, the Lestrygonians are a race of cannibal giants who capture and eat all of Odysseus's companions except for those on his own ship.

In Joyce's *Ulysses,* this episode is all about eating. We find Mr Bloom wandering round the streets of Dublin looking for somewhere to have lunch. But when he sees other people eating, he feels only disgust. The style is the now familiar interior monologue of Bloom. There is just one section, in the pub, when we hear other people talking about him in his absence. Otherwise, we accompany him as he roams the streets looking for a restaurant that doesn't induce nausea; we share his freely associating thoughts and listen to some conversations with people he meets.

Mostly this is very easy to follow; but I shall signpost a few references to his preoccupation with Molly and her would-be lover, Blazes Boylan, who is due to call on her at 4 o'clock.

As we begin the walk, Bloom is thinking about sugary treats, when *a sombre Y.M.C.A. man* hands him a throwaway (leaflet) about a visiting evangelist, Dr John Alexander Dowie. Then on p 191 he spots Dilly Dedalus (Simon Dedalus's 15-year-old daughter) and is saddened by her impoverished appearance *(Good Lord, that poor child's dress is in flitters.)* As he crosses O'Connell Bridge over the river Liffey he throws the screwed up leaflet at some seagulls. Later, he takes pity on their hunger and buys some cakes for them.

Near the bottom of p193, his mind turns to advertisements for 'clap' (sexual disease) clinics and then the horrid possibility occurs to him that Boylan might pass on a venereal disease to Molly:
Some chap with a dose burning him.
If he…
O!
Eh?
No…No.

And then: *think no more about that.* Instead, He thinks about Molly's witty remarks about Ben Dollard, the *bass barrel tone* singer.

The sight of five men carrying placards advertising Wisdom Hely's, the stationer (his former employer), evokes a stream of thought about advertising generally. This is followed (p 196) by a number of reminiscences about the earlier days of his marriage with Molly when their daughter Milly was little.

Then (197) he has a chance meeting with Mrs (Josie) Breen, an old friend of his and Molly's. She is worried about her husband who has bad dreams and is feeling persecuted as a result of a practical joke (a post card saying only: U.P.). They go on to talk about Mrs Mina Purefoy who has been in labour for 3 days in the lying-in hospital.

202 *He passed by the Irish Times*. And is reminded about his advertisement in that paper for '*a smart lady typist to aid gentleman in his literary work*'. This resulted in the response from Martha Clifford that he picked up at the post office in the 5th episode (Lotus Eaters). There are further musings about the travails of pregnant women before the sight of a squad of

policemen coming out from their lunch break reminds Bloom enviously of his hunger again (205). After some reflections on past encounters with policemen and informers, he has some rather depressing thoughts about the miseries of life and death. *This is the very worst hour of the day.* Next (209), he spots John Howard Parnell, the brother of the late Irish politician and folk hero, Charles Stewart Parnell. *There he is: the brother. Image of him.* Shortly afterwards he recognises the poet George (A E) Russell with his beard and bicycle accompanied by a young woman. Bloom muses about vegetarian food; then crosses at Nassau Street (211) and looks in the window of a shop selling field glasses. His thoughts run on astronomy, clocks and the exact meaning of 'parallax'. Bloom is always interested in science. But the thought of a full moon reminds him of a fortnight ago (*Wait. The full moon*...212), when he was walking by the river Tolka with Molly *and – he other side of her.* 'He', of course, is always Blazes Boylan though Bloom never mentions his name. Boylan was flirting: *Touch. Fingers. Asking. Answer. Yes.*

Stop. Stop. If it was it was. Must. (212)

213 Again he thinks about their early days, he and Molly. *I was happier then. Or was that I?*

This paragraph is full of longing and regret. *Could never like it (*sex*) again after Rudy.*

At last, he decides to go into a restaurant. He doesn't want to go home because that might mean a confrontation with Molly over her intention to be unfaithful with Boylan. But as soon as he opens the door of the Burton restaurant: *Stink gripped his trembling breath: pungent meat juice, slop of greens. See the animals feed.* (bottom of 214 to 216). We hear more, much more about the disgusting sights and smells of men eating. In the end, Bloom can't stand it and decides to leave. But vivid images of cannibalistic eating and butchery of animals follow him (and us) as he heads for Davy Byrne's pub (bottom line, 217).

Inside the pub, Bloom spends some time deciding what to order; and finally settles on a glass of red wine (burgundy) and a gorgonzola cheese sandwich. An acquaintance (Nosey Flynn) asks about Molly (*wife well?*) (219). Bloom tells Flynn about her forthcoming singing tour. Flynn says *'Isn't Blazes Boylan mixed up in it?'* reminding Bloom yet again of her forthcoming afternoon tryst.

Davy Byrne, the landlord, joins them and Flynn asks if has a tip *(a good one)* for the Gold Cup race at Ascot later in the day. But Davy Byrne is no longer a betting man. Further ruminations about meat-eating and butchery follow. However, Bloom is now able to find eating amusing rather than disgusting (223) and imagines being a waiter in a posh restaurant. (*Do ptake some ptarmigan*).

223 (4 lines from bottom) *Two flies stuck...*The sight of two buzzing flies stuck together (mating) on a window pane takes him back to the first time he and Molly made love – in the open air, on Howth Head (pronounced *Hoath* Head), a high grassy headland on the coast of Dublin Bay. He recalls that joyous, passionate day in a passage of great poetic and erotic power (224).

When Bloom's bladder tells him he needs to visit the outdoor lavatory, he goes through the door leaving Nosey Flynn and Davy Byrne to speculate about this odd person in his absence. *What is this is he? Isn't he in the insurance line?* (half-way down 225). He's in 'the craft' (the freemasons) they think: 226). But (lower down 226 and 227) they concede that he has his good points too.

On P 229, Bloom is feeling better thanks to his glass of wine. He hums the aria from Mozart's *Don Giovanni* which will feature in Molly's concert tour. Still in a good mood, he helps a blind young man across the road, and tries to imagine what it would be like to be deprived of vision. Then (234) he has a quick glimpse of Boylan : *Straw hat in sunlight. Tan shoes Turned-up trousers. It is. It is.* Quickly, he avoids contact with the Seducer and strides hurriedly towards the National Museum, where he intends to examine the statues of Greek goddesses to see whether they have an anus. The end of the gastro-intestinal tract.

Notes on Episode 9: SCYLLA AND CHARYBDIS (235-280)

Time 2 p.m. Place: The National Library

In Homer, Odysseus and his men are warned to avoid the twin perils of Scylla and Charybdis by steering careful in between them. Scylla is a monster who sits on a rock and snatches people to devour; Charybdis is a whirlpool. In Joyce's version they might be the contrasting arguments of Plato and Aristotle, with the conventional librarians representing the whirling abstractions of Plato and the more analytical style of Aristotle whom Joyce greatly admired.

In this episode we find ourselves in the National Library where Stephen Dedalus is having a discussion about Shakespeare with Mr Lyster the librarian. (*Urbane, to comfort them, the quaker librarian purred*). Also present are another librarian and writer, John Eglinton (real name: William Magee), and the philosopher A E Russell (all real people).

Stephen is anxious to make an impression on these gentlemen so that he can gain a place for himself in Dublin's literary world. He is doing this by telling them about his theory of the way Shakespeare's personal life was a major influence on his work. The others disagree vigorously.

Sometimes Stephen doesn't speak out loud but rehearses his arguments to himself. We can tell when he is talking, rather than just thinking, because of the initial dash – which Joyce uses to indicate speech. Some paragraphs are devoted to his stream of thoughts. These are full of obscure references and very difficult to understand! I recommend that you read them for the fleeting visions they produce and don't try to understand them exactly. It is better to follow the thread of the Shakespeare discussion which will carry you safely through.

The conversation is interrupted by the arrival of Buck Mulligan in his usual mischievous mood – and later resumed. Finally Stephen and Mulligan leave together, encountering Bloom on the way.

The first few pages are difficult: but press on! *Cranly* is Stephen's medical student friend from his days in Paris: the bawdy verse belongs to him. The quotation beginning *Orchestral Satan* starts with Milton's *Paradise Lost* and the last (rude) line is from Dante. The Shakespeare discussion begins midway on 236 (*Our young Irish bards*). On p 237 they are joined by Mr Best, the deputy librarian. *Mr Best entered, tall, young, mild, light.* Stephen counters the vague generalisations of his opponents with crisp examples of the ways the author's life experiences have, in his view, been translated into his art. Eglinton (a Platonist) gets angry when Stephen is revealed as an Aristotle champion (238 *Upon my word it makes my blood boil...*).

On p240 (last para), Stephen launches his lecture with an imagined portrayal of the first performance of Hamlet: *It is this hour of day in mid June, Stephen said, begging with a swift glance their hearing.* He goes on to argue that Shakespeare identified Hamlet's murdered father with himself, suggesting that his wife Ann Hathaway (whom he left in Stratford for 30 years when he went to London) was unfaithful to him and destroyed his (sexual) self-confidence. (*Belief in himself has been untimely killed.*)

Russell says that Shakespeare's private life is of no importance (242) *I mean when we read the poetry of King Lear what is it to us how the poet lived?* The argument continues with interpolations of Stephen's private thoughts:

242 *How now, sirrah, that pound he lent you?* Stephen remembers that Russell once lent him a pound which he spent on a prostitute called Georgina Johnson. The others have a more benign view of Ann Hathaway: but Stephen reminds them of the young men being seduced by older women in Shakespeare's work.

On page 245, Russell says he has to leave and there is the first mention of a literary gathering to which everyone except Stephen has been invited. Even Mulligan and Haines, his fellow tenants in the Martello tower will be going. The others go on talking about the forthcoming party until Russell departs and the librarian takes up the Shakespearean thread again: *Is it your view, then, that she was not faithful to the poet?* (247). Stephen muses to himself about Shakespeare's love life and the ambience of the library reading room (*Coffined thoughts around me in mummy cases* 248). The quaker librarian speaks hopefully of 'reconciliation' between Shakespeare and Ann; Stephen goes on to remind them of the daughters lost and then found in the later plays (*What softens the heart of a man...?* 250) He references Marina in *Pericles*, Miranda (*a wonder*) in *The Tempest* and Perdita in *The Winter's Tale*.

The discussion continues at some length and, rather than overburden you with detail here, I would recommend that you simply read it and make what you can of it.

It is interrupted when the voice of Stephen's friend/enemy, Buck Mulligan announces his arrival (*Amen! responded from the doorway*) and we have an *Entr'acte* (Bottom of 252)

Mulligan, characteristically, refuses to take the debate seriously and is more concerned with taking Stephen to task for failing to turn up at the pub for lunch as promised and sending a telegram instead. He does this in a mock Irish accent, imitating the style of a J M Synge play, rudely ignoring the others (255, bottom). A telegram was a rapid printed message sent telegraphically via a post office, before the age of electronic 'texts'.

Another interruption follows (bottom of 256) this time from an attendant, telling Mr Lyster, the librarian: *There's a gentleman here, sir...From the Freeman.* The gentleman is Mr Bloom who makes the first of two fleeting appearances in this episode. Note that he is a complete outsider here and we see *him* only through the eyes of the others: *a bowing dark figure following his* (the librarian's) *hasty heels.* (257) Bloom has just come from the adjacent Museum where he has been checking to see if the Greek goddesses have anuses. They don't.

On p 258, the Shakespeare debate gets going again (*We want to hear more)*.Stephen produces more speculative tales of the Bard's love life. He maintains that Ann, the older woman, seduced William into marriage, and then betrayed him with his brother. The company go on to chew over the vexed question of the 'second best bed' which was all that William chose to bequeath his widow in his will. This leads to a general vilification of Shakespeare's character including rather anti-semitic charges that he was, or might have been, Jewish.

At the bottom of p 265 the subject changes to the position of fathers. *A father, Stephen said, battling against hopelessness, is a necessary evil. His only connection with his son is a single sex act.* He goes on to claim that that Shakespeare's brothers, Edmund and Richard both appear in the plays as villains. If they also slept with Ann while Shakespeare was in London one of them may have been the father of William's son, Hamnet (whose name is almost Hamlet).

The plot thickens says John Eglinton and indeed the narrative style turns into a play script for a page and a half.

We may wonder what all this convoluted literary argument has to do with the plot of *Ulysses* and what part it plays in telling us more about the relationships between the three main characters, Stephen, Bloom and Molly. The answer may be that Shakespeare contained in his imagination *both* Hamlet the son and his ghostly father. Shakespeare's little son Hamnet died at the age of 11 and Bloom's wife, Molly is betraying him with Blazes Boylan, just as, in the play, Gertrude betrays Hamlet's father with Claudius. These correspondences run through the chapter, while Bloom himself pops up twice to remind us of his existence.

Stephen plunges on with his exposition, with only short interruptions. Until (274), when Eglinton bluntly asks, '*Do you believe your own theory?*' To which Stephen answers, '*No*'. There is a brief conversation about payments for articles and then Mulligan calls on '*Kinch*' (his nickname for Stephen) to leave with him. The others talk about 'seeing you tonight' (but Stephen has not been invited). Stephen and Mulligan talk as they walk through the reading room to the outside. Mulligan reads the cast list of an obscene play he says he has written. As they reach the main door, Stephen senses someone behind him and stops to let him pass: it is Bloom once again.

279 Stephen's decision to break off his relationship with Mulligan is anticipated by the sight of Bloom (*Part. The moment is now:* 12 lines from the top.) and he appears to recall a dream he had last night (in Episode 3, Proteus pp. 58-9) foreseeing events in later episodes when Bloom escorts him safely away from the brothel (*Street of harlots after*) and offers to introduce him to Molly (*A cream-fruit melon he held to me. You will see.*) The young Stephen (like the young Joyce) will mature and become someone with the sensibilities of Bloom.

The wandering jew, Buck Mulligan whispered with clown's awe. He makes further whispered fun of Bloom. *A dark back* (Bloom's) *went before them.*

The episode ends with a quotation from the final lines of Shakespeare's *Cymbeline*.

You have now read, and at least partially understood, the episode that has been described as the most intellectually challenging in the book. Well done!

The next one is much easier.

Notes on Episode 10: WANDERING ROCKS (280-328)

Time: 3 to 4 p.m. Place: the streets of Dublin.

The Wandering Rocks are only briefly mentioned by Homer as a hazard to shipping.

This is the central episode of *Ulysses* (though well short of the half-way point for the reader). The style is third-person description by an omniscient narrator with spoken dialogue. We also share the thoughts of some of the other characters as well as Bloom.

Unlike all the other episodes, this one is divided into 19 sections, mostly short, and separated by a horizontal bar. I have numbered them 1 to 19. It might help to pencil in the numbers. The narration moves all over the centre of Dublin observing the activities of different characters in the same hour.

1. (280) We follow the progress of the very reverend John Conmee, the Jesuit superior of St Francis Xavier Church*. He encounters a number of Dublin citizens including: a one-legged sailor; the wife of Mr David Sheehy M.P; three schoolboys; and Mr Denis J Maginni, professor of dancing. Along North Strand Road, he passes shops, a pub and a funeral establishment. At Newcomen Bridge, he boards a tramcar and rides as far as Howth Road. Walking through a field, he reads from his breviary, a little late, the office of *Nones.* His thoughts range widely; yet he observes everyone, saying a few words to some. A young couple emerge, flustered from a gap in a hedge.

The young woman abruptly bent and detached from her light skirt a clinging twig. Father Conmee interrupts, briefly, his reading from his prayer book to bless them both.

*Father Conmee was a real person who was rector of Clongowes Wood College in Dublin where Joyce went to school. He appears also in Joyce's first novel, *Portrait of the Artist as a Young Man*. Here, Stephen Dedalus is also a pupil at Clongowes and the kindly Father Conmee saves him from an unjust caning.

2. (288) Corny Kelleher is the undertaker whom we met at Paddy Dignam's funeral (episode 6 HADES). His conferring with a policeman confirms Bloom's opinion that he is an informer. *A generous white arm* flinging a coin (to the one-legged sailor), belongs, as we shall see, to Molly Bloom.

3. (288) And here comes that sailor on his crutch. His growls of *For England Home and Beauty* as he begs for money, remind us that he will have served in the British Navy. The last paragraph confirms that the *plump bare, generous arm* flinging him the coin is Molly's.

4. (289) We are in the kitchen of the Dedalus family home. Stephen's younger sisters are hungry because their mother is dead and their father, Simon Dedalus (modelled on Joyce's father), is not providing enough money to buy food. Katey Dedalus has even tried, unsuccessfully, to sell some of her older brother's books.

Note that this section, like all the others, contains little inserts to remind us what people in the other sections are doing. In this one we get a quick glance back at Fr Conmee (top of 290) and check the progress down the river of Blooms's discarded evangelical leaflet (*a crumpled throwaway, Elijah is coming*) in the last paragraph.

5. (291) Here we watch Blazes Boylan buying a present of fruit for Molly Bloom whom he is due to visit at 4 o'clock. And flirting with the salesgirl.

6. (292) Near Trinity College, Stephen encounters his old singing teacher, Almidano Artifoni, who tries to encourage him to persevere with a musical career...

7. (293) Miss Dunne is Blazes Boylan's secretary. She is trying to type a letter but gets as only as far as the date (16 June 1904) reminding us of the date on which *Ulysses* is set. She is interrupted by a phone call from her boss.

8. (295) We are in the historic council chamber of St Mary's Abbey, with Ned Lambert and the clergyman when J J (Jack) Molloy the cash-strapped barrister comes into the dark room, shining his torch on their faces. Note the 'flashback' to the same time but a different place where the young woman is detaching a clinging twig from her skirt (section 1). When the clergyman has gone, Ned and Molloy leave together and Ned starts sneezing before Molloy can speak (no doubt, to ask for a loan).

9. (297) Tom Rochford is demonstrating to Lenehan and McCoy a machine he has invented to show the number of the act which is currently on stage in a music hall. As they leave the theatre, Lenehan shows McCoy a manhole down which Tom Rochford bravely descended to rescue someone overcome by gas in the sewer. The conversation between them turns to racing and Lenehan says that he met *Bantam Lyons going to back a bloody horse that hasn't got an earthly*. Lyons says that the tip was given him by Bloom. But, we know that there was no tip. In episode 5 (The Lotus Eaters), Bloom gave Lyons a newspaper saying that he was going to throw it away anyhow; Lyons thought this was a sly tip for a horse called 'Throwaway'. And in fact a horse called Throwaway did win the Gold Cup race at Ascot on 16 June 1904!

Then they catch sight of Bloom himself: *a darkbacked figure scanning books on a hawker's cart*. McCoy mentions Bloom's interest in astronomy and (300) Lenehan is reminded of an evening when he shared a car (a horse-drawn jaunting car) with the Blooms. While sitting next to Molly, he took advantage with her full consent (he boasts), of the opportunity to fondle her breasts. Meanwhile, Bloom was discoursing on stars and comets and oblivious of what was going on in the seat behind. Lenehan collapses with laughter at his own story; but then he becomes more serious and pays tribute to Bloom:
- *He's a cultured allroundman Bloom is... He's not one of your common or garden... you*

know… There's a touch of the artist about old Bloom.

10. (302) We now move over to Bloom's point of view as he browses the bookstalls, looking for the sort of book that Molly might enjoy. After sampling a number of mildly pornographic novelettes, he settles for *Sweets of Sin.*

11. (304) Outside the auction rooms, Dilly, the eldest Dedalus girl, catches her errant father as he comes round the corner. She suspects (rightly), that he has got hold of a little money and tries to get him to give her a few shillings of it to buy food for the family. At first he is amused but later becomes angry as she insists that he has more shillings than he is willing to admit.

12. (307) Tom Kernan, a rather self-satisfied commercial traveller (first encountered at Dignam's funeral) walks along, encountering a number of other minor characters. He congratulates himself on his business acumen and his smart appearance. He notes the spot where Robert Emmet, the 1803 revolutionary was hanged; and savours the residual effects of the gin he has recently imbibed. He is passed by the tail end of a cavalcade of carriages with outriders. This is the procession of the Lord Lieutenant or Governor General of Ireland, of which we get fleeting glimpses in several sections and a full description in the final one.

13. (310) Stephen Dedalus is looking at a lapidary (jewelry worker) polishing a chain behind his shop window. This evokes all sorts of thoughts about the provenance of precious stones.

   He moves on to Bedford Row with its bookstalls, where he is recognised by his sister, Dilly, (see 11.)He notes *Dilly's high shoulders and shabby dress.* Dilly has just bought a tattered French language primer for a penny. She is embarrassed when Stephen asks her if she intends to learn French. (She has ambitions too.) His sister confirms that since he left home they have had to pawn some of his books in order to survive. Stephen feels a pang of conscience, or in Joyce's antique phrase*: agenbite of inwit* (313).He should have stayed to support them. But if he goes back*: she will drown me with her, eyes and hair.*

14. (313) Now we are observing a meeting between Mr Dedalus senior and the rather hapless Father Cowley, a former priest who has fallen from the Church but is not excommunicated.

   Father Cowley is in trouble; two debt-collectors are *prowling around the house trying to effect an entrance.* He is waiting for his friend, Ben Dollard, (famous for his 'base barreltone' singing voice). Ben has promised to say a word to 'Long John' the Dublin Subsheriff who will be able to get the moneylender off his back. Happily for Father Cowley, Ben has discovered that Cowley's landlord has already distrained for rent and so, in law, he has a prior claim on any money or goods that might be available.

15. (316) *The youngster will be alright*, says Martin Cunningham (see episode 6, HADES). He is referring to the late Paddy Dignam's little boy, for whom he is seeking subscriptions to set up a charitable fund. A group of male Dublin citizens collects at the City Hall where they meet 'Long John' Fanning, the Subsheriff (who has never heard of Dignam) and try to interest him in supporting the fund. We hear that Bloom has put his name down for five shillings *and paid it too. There is much kindness in the jew,* says John Wyse Nolan: a quotation from Shakespeare's *The Merchant of Venice* and another slightly ironic compliment for Bloom.

    In this episode, there are several passing references to other characters we have met, or will soon meet.

    At line 7, we are told about *Bronze and Gold, Miss Kennedy's head by Miss Douce's head*. These attractive heads belong to the two barmaids in the Ormond Hotel whom we will find dispensing drinks in the next episode. Blazes Boylan is also spotted again (317), and finally, the group of men outside the City Hall hear the *Clatter of horsehoofs* and turn to see the procession of the Lord Lieutenant passing by.

16. (319) Buck Mulligan and Haines (the Englishman staying with Mulligan and Stephen in the Martello Tower in the first episode) are going to have tea in the Dublin Bakery Company café.

    They discuss Stephen in a disparaging way. *He is going to write something in ten years*, says Mulligan, laughing. Joyce is also having a laugh because the something *he* is going to write in ten years is the book we are reading now.

In the last paragraph, we see that the Elijah leaflet that Bloom threw into the Liffey has now reached Dublin Bay and completed its journey.

17. (321) We observe the singing teacher, Almido Artifoni, and also Cashel Boyle O'Connor Fitzgerald, the deranged man who walks round lampposts. Here he collides with the blind stripling who curses him fiercely. *God's curse on you whoever you are, he said sourly. You're blinder nor I am, you bitch's bastard!*

    You may be puzzled by the reference *to Bloom's dental windows.* The dentist is no relation of our friend, Leopold. It's just that there really was a dentist called Bloom in Dublin and Joyce borrowed his name for the book.

18. (322) Here we see Patrick Aloysius Dignam, bereaved son of the late Patrick Dignam, coming back from the butcher's with some pork steaks, as instructed.

    He sees an advertisement for a boxing match (a 'pucker' is a boxer), and he muses about famous pugilists like Fitzsimons and Corbett. He passes Blazes Boylan (*a red flower in a toff's mouth and a swell pair of kicks (*shoes) *on him*). Then he remembers the appearance of his father after death. (*His face got all grey...* (323), his last words to his son, and the events before and after the death. *Pa was inside it* (the coffin) *and ma crying in the parlour...* We feel very sad for him.

19. (324) At last we are told that the magnificent procession of horse-drawn carriages is escorting The Lord Lieutenant (or Governor-General) of Ireland, the earl of Dudley, and Lady Dudley, across the city from Phoenix Park in the North, over the river Liffey to Ringsend in the South where they are going to open a bazaar. The final section presents a sort of speeded-up version of the whole chapter as, from the point of view of those in the carriages, we see in rapid succession, all the people already described (including Bronze and Gold, the barmaids at the Ormond Hotel), and a few more for good measure.

PS After completing this episode, if your eyes should stray to the first 3 pages of the next Episode ('Sirens') and you feel overcome with dismay because it seems to be in code – be of good cheer! All will be become completely clear in due course.

Notes on Episode 11: SIRENS (328 - 376)

The place: The Ormond Hotel. Time: 4 p.m.

In Homer, Odysseus and his men avoid the fatal temptation of the seductive and dangerous voices of the Sirens.: his men plug their ears with wax and Odysseus has himself tied to the mast so that he can hear the song but is unable to give himself up to the singers.

Introduction We are in the bar of the Ormond Hotel on the North bank of Dublin's river Liffey. The sirens are the two barmaids, Miss Douce (bronze hair), and Miss Kennedy, (blonde/gold hair). They have heard the ringing hoofbeats of the viceregal cavalcade in the previous episode. Or as Joyce puts in in the first line of 'Sirens': *Bronze by Gold heard the hoofirons steelyrining.* This chapter is Joyce's attempt to represent the language of music in words. It is full of short phrases: repeated, varied, chopped up and assorted; rising and falling lines; melodies and dissonances, pianissimos and crashing climaxes; recurring leitmotifs. The voices that we hear are those of a narrator and the speech of the characters with interpolations from Bloom's thoughts.

When you read the first three pages for the first time you will be mystified. This doesn't matter. It is a kind of overture or perhaps a rehearsal in which we hear, in sequence, snatches of all the main themes and climaxes in the episode to come. Read it and just enjoy the music. The 'overture' ends, and the episode proper begins at the bottom of page 330 with the words: *Done. Begin!* When you have finished the rest of the chapter, read the 'overture' again and, as a summary, it will make complete sense. Now we shall begin:

Page 331. The two barmaids, Miss Douce and Miss Kennedy, alias Bronze and Gold, have been gazing at the viceregal procession through the window and taking an interest in the posh people in the front carriages. They complain about the impertinence *(imperthnthn)* of the boot boy as he brings them their tea and they talk about Miss Douce's holiday. They remember asking for some skin lotion from an old fogey in Boyd's the chemist (331) and go into shrieks of laughter at the idea of being married to this old man with his greasy skin. Bloom, who, for some time has been just outside the Ormond, overhears the girls and thinks they must be talking about him. He walks away from the hotel: *By Cantwell's offices roved Greasabloom* (335, middle). He is thinking about that advertisement for Mr Keyes and also looking for somewhere to eat.

Some regular customers now saunter into the Ormond and chat up the barmaids. There's Simon Dedalus (335) who is gallantly flirtatious, followed by Lenehan (last para, 336) who has come to meet Boylan. Lenehan tells Simon about Stephen's performance in the Library earlier in the afternoon. But Simon Dedalus does not seem very interested in his son's fame. He notes that the piano has been moved into the saloon bar and is told that the blind young piano-tuner has been to attend to it. Mr Dedalus goes over to the piano, lifts the lid and tries out its newly-tuned notes.

Meanwhile, Bloom having reached nearby Essex Bridge (339), remembers he has to pop into Hely's the stationer to buy paper and envelopes (*two sheets of cream vellum paper*), to reply to his letter from Martha, his secret correspondent from Chapter 5 (Lotus-eaters). Suddenly, Bloom spots Blazes Boylan driving in a pony and trap (jaunting car), heading for the Ormond. He decides to follow him in (discreetly).

He eyed and saw afar on Essex Bridge a gay hat riding on a jaunting car. It is. Third time. Coincidence. Jingling on supple rubbers is jaunted from the bridge to Ormond quay. Follow. Risk it. Go quick. Near Now. At four. Out.

Repeated references to *Jingle,* signal the sound of Boylan's jaunting car in the street; or just in Bloom's thoughts. *At four* reminds us that Bloom is painfully conscious of Boylan's forthcoming appointment with Molly which is at 4 p.m.

In the saloon bar (340) everyone now hears Simon Dedalus singing 'Goodbye, Sweetheart, Goodbye' of which the first line is *The bright stars fade;* and accompanying himself on the piano.

Reaching the hotel, Boylan goes in to the bar while Bloom follows him at a distance, not to be seen.

341 Bloom meets Richie Goulding, the lawyers' bookkeeper, and decides to join him for an early dinner in the dining room. Meanwhile Lenehan and Boylan are occupied with the barmaids and Miss Douce is persuaded to do her famous garter trick – *Sonnezlacloche!)* (343). Then, suddenly, it's time for Boylan to stride off in his creaking shoes to his date with Molly Bloom.

344 Now two more men come into the bar for a drink. They are Ben Dollard who we know has a very good bass voice and Father Cowley whom we also met in the last chapter.

Meanwhile, in the adjacent dining room, 'Bald Pat', the 'bothered' waiter, is taking orders for drinks from Bloom and Richie Goulding.

Ben Dollard and Cowley join Simon Dedalus round the piano and reminisce about an evening when Ben was due to perform in a concert but had no 'wedding garment' and had to borrow a suit from the Blooms who, at that time, were supplementing their income with a second-hand clothes business (*Mrs Marion Bloom has left off clothes of all descriptions*, 346).

Meanwhile, we cut between scenes of Boylan jingling along to his tryst and Bloom and Richie, in the dining room, eating their dinner, attended by bald, deaf Pat.

349 Father Cowley sits at the piano and plays a few notes. He is a really good pianist. He and Ben Dollard try to persuade Simon Dedalus to sing one of his party pieces, the aria *M'Appari* from the opera *Martha* by Friedrich Flotow.

352 Eventually, with Fr Cowley accompanying him on the piano, he sings the aria in which the tenor hero is grief-stricken at having had to part with Martha, the girl he loves. Bloom and Richie Goulding listen from the adjoining room with the door left open.

As Bloom listens to this highly charged, passionate song, *M'appari tutt amor* (350) his heart is wrung by thoughts of his loss of Molly (to Boylan). Later, we are given lines from the English version: *When first I saw that form endearing...* The climax of the song is beautifully rendered in Joyce's words *(It soared like a bird* ...355). We should, if possible, listen to the song on the CD of Songs from or associated with Joyce's novels (if still available), while we read Joyce's description. Or any other recording.

The narrative continues to cross-cut in a cinematic way between the singing in the Ormond Saloon, Bloom and Richie in the dining room, Boylan's inexorable journey towards the Bloom house in Eccles Street and the conversation of the barmaids with their customers in the bar.

360 Bloom tries to distract himself by composing a letter to his fantasy love, the pseudonymous Martha (the same name as the heroine of the Flotow opera). He tries out phrases which mingle in his mind with fragments from her letter to him. And observations about bald Pat, the waiter.

364 last three lines: *One rapped on a door.* Now Bloom imagines he can hear Boylan knocking on the door of his house. Knock rhymes with cock (Boylan's) and Paul de Kock (the author of sexy books).

365 Ben Dollard's rich bass voice is heard singing the solemn and much loved folk song, *The Croppy Boy.* This tells the story of a young Irish rebel who confesses to a priest who reveals himself to be an English soldier in disguise. The Croppy Boy is arrested and hanged. Everyone is listening intently, even the barmaids. It's another story of betrayal, fitting in too well with Bloom's plight; he decides to leave before the end.

Two more motifs now intersperse the main theme. One is the tapping sound (*Tap. Tap.*), of the blind stripling piano tuner who seems to be identified with the tragic Croppy Boy. The other is the *cockcarracarra* sound of Boylan's insolent sexuality. All the themes merge and mingle as we hear them and we see the montage of images they evoke in Bloom's mind. Including memories of Molly.

372 *Gassy thing that cider:* Out in the street now, Bloom is beginning to feel full of gas. Perhaps it's the burgundy he had at lunchtime. He encounters a prostitute (*a frowzy whore with black straw sailor hat askew)*, whom he thinks had been a friend of Molly (374). Looking into the window of an antique shop (375) he sees a picture of Robert Emmet, another Irish rebel hero who led a pathetic little rebellion in 1803 and was later tried and executed (hanged for treason), in Dublin. The first part of his inspiring speech in the dock comes in to Bloom's mind *When my country takes her place among the free nations of the world, then and not till then, let my epitaph be written.* Mr Bloom finally lets out a fart, which relieves his intestinal bloating and perhaps expresses his contempt for the sentimental way in which many Irishmen dwell on the nationalist martyrs of the past and their failed attempts to gain their country's freedom.

Notes on Episode 12: CYCLOPS (376-449)

In Homer, Odysseus and his companions find themselves imprisoned in the cave of Polyphemus, the one-eye giant cyclops, prior to being eaten by the monster. Odysseus blinds the giant with a brand from the fire, thrust in to his single eye; and they all escape, each tied to the underbelly of a sheep.

The narrator of this episode is an un-named man who is clearly one of the layabouts rather than the intellectuals. His impromptu storytelling is alternated with a series of contrasting versions of the events which echo and make fun of the preceding narrative. They seem to be the voice of someone (James Joyce) who can parody a variety of grand styles. These passages may seem out of proportion: clumsy giants like the Cyclops. You may feel irritation with them and want to get on with the 'real' story. However if you have patience, you will find them surprisingly entertaining!

Here is our main narrator:

376. I was just passing the time of day with old Troy of the D.M.P at the corner of Arbour Hill there and be damned but a bloody sweep came along and he near drove his gear into my eye.

The D.M.P. stands for Dublin Metropolitan Police. The near-accident to the narrator's eye is regarded as a passing reference to the blinding of the Cyclops in *The Odyssey*. The narrator's current job is to be a collector of bad debts and, when he encounters his friend Joe Hynes, he tells Joe how he has been trying to get some money owed to his client, Moses Herzog, for unpaid grocery bills. This paragraph contains the first of many casual antisemitic utterances in the Cyclops episode. It is followed by an account, in obscure legal language, of the debtor's misdemeanours.

The two men decide to go to Barney Kiernan's Pub to slake their thirst (378, last para). The subject of trade evokes an interpolation in the form of an elaborate account of a sort of legendary land of plenty. *In Inisfail the fair there lies a land*... This leads to the description of a huge and magnificent market full of vegetable produce and live, bellowing animals.

In the pub (bottom of 380) Joe and the narrator find 'the citizen', a rather scary, bigoted old republican with fierce revolutionary views, accompanied by his decrepit old dog, Garryowen. Drinks are ordered and there is some general conversation about the state of the world.

On pages 382-384, we get a wonderful parody of the citizen in the language of folk legends: *The figure seated on a large boulder at the foot of a round tower...* This is very entertaining and includes the first of Joyce's long lists of names, this time of *Irish heroes and heroines of antiquity.* If you take the trouble to read all the names you will find that Joyce mischievously slips in all sorts of other celebrities who were definitely not Irish folk heroes.

Terry, the barman, comes round with three pints (384) and Joe pays with a sovereign (a pound), remarking that there's more where that came from thanks to a racing tip from *the prudent member* (meaning Bloom). The citizen reads out from a newspaper the list of births, deaths and marriages. He complains that in this supposedly Irish newspaper all the names are of people in England.

The high-flown style of the second narrator tells us that *as they quaffed their cup of joy, a godlike messenger came swiftly in.* (385). This is only the unprepossessing little Alf Bergan who has seen poor old Denis Breen, the recipient of the anonymous 'U.P.' letter, hurrying to yet another solicitor to take out an action for £10,000. And pursued by his wife, Molly's friend, Josie. (See episode 8, Lestrygonians).

Alf shouts at Terry to bring drinks for him and his friend, Bob Doran, who is discovered, already drunk and slouched in the corner. This rouses the alternate narrator to describe the serving of drinks in a totally inappropriate epic style, culminating in a paean to Queen Victoria (387).

The citizen irritably remarks on *that bloody freemason… prowling up and down outside?* (387).

This is, of course, Bloom, who, as we shall see, is waiting to meet Martin Cunningham on an errand of mercy to the bereaved Dignam family. 'Freemason' is uses as a code word for Jew, since all Jews are suspected of being members of the organisation.

There is a little confusion about whether Paddy Dignam is dead or not (Alf claims to have seen him in the street 'just now'). The alternate narrator butts in (389) with an account of a séance in which contact is made with the spirit of the recently buried Dignam. *(In the darkness spirit hands…).*

Back in the pub, Bob Doran starts up a loud drunken lament for Dignam, to the disgust of the others.

Bloom now returns, looking for Martin Cunningham, and hovers near the door, eliciting a growl from Garryowen, clearly an antisemitic dog.

Come in, come on, he won't eat you, says the citizen (bottom of 391).

392 Joe Hynes starts to read out some letters that Alf has got hold of which were apparently written by hangmen. The company are intrigued by the mention of a post-mortem erection which Bloom tries to explain physiologically (bottom of 393: *That can be explained by science, says Bloom).* For this, he is mocked by the alternate narrator (393-394).

394 Bob Doran teases the dog *(Give us the paw!)* to the disgust of the narrator who then reports that Bloom and the citizen are having an argument about the 1798 rebellion (395). The narrator tells a tale about Bloom which puts him in a poor light and the citizen starts to get more hostile to him.

396 He seems to be reproaching Bloom for a lack of respect for the dead revolutionaries and this results in a long and hilariously absurd account of the scene preceding the execution of an Irish rebel which goes on for several pages. When the pub discussion is resumed (402) the subjects are the Irish language, 'antitreating' (a clearly useless plan to reduce alcohol consumption) and the humane treatment of dogs. This, the alternate narrator claims (in the style of a newspaper article), could even lead to the dog, Garryowen, being able to recite ancient verses in a sort of canine Celtic!

The conversations ramble on as the drinking continues; and the alternate narrator continues to introduce his highly wrought illustrations. It is not too difficult to distinguish between the two styles.

The next topic (405) is the plight of Paddy Dignam's widow and the problems around her late husband's insurance policy which Bloom and Martin Cunningham will try to sort out for her. Bloom makes a slip saying *the wife's admirers* instead of *the wife's advisers*: clearly thinking of Molly and her admirers.

406 Bob Doran gets more and more drunk and we finally see him staggering out towards home as the others enjoy a story about him getting robbed by a prostitute while in a similar state. The drinkers then consider the Foot and Mouth disease problem. The narrator describes Bloom's habit of giving unsolicited advice about the care of animals. However, he says, Bloom would *have a soft hand under a hen. Ga Ga Gara. Klook Klook Klook* (2/3 down 408). We are then treated to parody of a Westminster parliamentary debate about Foot and Mouth Disease (409).

It emerges (410) that the citizen was a champion shot putter in his young days and this leads to a discussion of traditional Irish sports (410-412) and the description of a boxing match in the style of a popular sports reporter (412). The atmosphere becomes increasingly violent from now on.

There is further curiosity about Molly's concert tour with Boylan; aimed, as usual, at discomfiting poor Bloom. Then (bottom of 414) Ned Lambert and J.J. (Jack) Molloy join the company and more drinks are ordered. The talk turns again to Mr Breen who is now looking for a private detective in his deranged attempts to sue whoever sent him the anonymous note that read only 'U.P.' Everyone regards Breen with derision, but Mr Bloom expresses pity for his wife (416).

On 417 (half way down) Joe asks *How did the Canada Swindle case go off?* It appears that a Jew (*One of the bottlenosed fraternity*) has swindled a fellow Jew and the judge shows sympathy for the plaintiff and his large family. This leads to thinly disguised antisemitic grumbling from the citizen.

John Wyse Nolan and Lenehan then come in (bottom of 420), and Nolan reports a debate in the city hall about the revival of the Irish language.

The surprise result of the Ascot Gold Cup race is briefly pondered (422). The citizen makes a long speech (about how Ireland used to be a powerfully productive trading nation before the British colonisation (reminiscent of the more recent arguments about 'Brexit'). When John Wyse (Nolan) remarks that Ireland is losing her trees, (*As treeless as Portugal we'll be soon*, bottom of 423) the alternate narrator produces a wonderful account (perhaps his best) of a wedding in which all concerned, including the happy couple and their very long list of guests, appear to be different species of trees!

After this sylvan interlude the tone again becomes violent. There is an account of the brutal punishments inflicted in the British Navy (bottom of 426). This leads to a tirade against the British by the citizen culminating in a call for all the expatriate Irish people to return and take vengeance on their British masters.

Everyone (except Bloom) joins in a chorus of vilification of the other European nations.

Bottom of 429: Another round of drinks is requested. Meanwhile *Bloom was talking and talking with John Wyse* about persecution (430):
Persecution, says he, all the history of the world is full of it. Perpetuating national hatred among nations.
There is a brief discussion about what a nation is, until the citizen addresses Bloom:
What is your nation, if I may ask, says the citizen.
Bloom tells him: *Ireland*, and the citizen spits theatrically. The other narrator intervenes with a digression about the 'ancient Irish facecloth', as if I trying to cool the situation down. It is too late, because the citizen's hostility to Bloom is now coming out into the open. But it is Bloom who now, with considerable courage, raises the tension even further (bottom of 431).

And I belong to a race too, says Bloom that is hated and persecuted. Also now. This very moment. This very instant.
And a little later: *But it's no use, says he. Force, hatred, history, all that.*
That's not life for men and women. Insult and hatred. Mr Bloom is talking about Love. Then he hastily apologises and rushes off to keep his appointment with Martin Cunningham.
In his absence, the citizen talks about the hypocrisy of preachers, and especially those colonial invaders who talked about the love of God but used brutal force to subdue the natives. Then, suddenly (435) Lenehan announces that Bloom has gone to collect his winnings

from the surprise victory, at odds of 20 to 1, in the Gold Cup race, of the horse called Throwaway. Lenehan believes that Bloom gave this tip to Bantam Lyons earlier in the day, but we know that all he said is that he was going to 'throw away' his newspaper and has won no money whatsoever. The narrator now leaves to seek the toilet and empty his bladder, *(round to the back of the yard to pumpship* 435, last para) muttering to himself about the cunning and deceitfulness of Bloom. When he comes back, the antisemitic fever is mounting, with Bloom (and his father before him), darkly accused of all sorts of misdemeanours.

Martin Cunningham turns up with two friends, looking for Bloom (436). Their arrival is celebrated by the other narrator with a delightful mock-medieval parody. *Our travellers reached the rustic hostelry and alighted from their palfreys (*436-7*).* Meanwhile, in the pub, all sorts of insults and abusive lies are now being exchanged about Bloom. He is a fake messiah, a coward, not a real man, and probably not the real father of his children, being incapable of sexual intercourse.

Martin Cunningham, much more decent and fair-minded than the others, protests mildly and asks for *Charity to the neighbour* (439) and says *God bless all is my prayer* (440). The citizen says *Amen* and the other narrator comes in with a lengthy description of an epic religious ceremony attended by (among many others) saints, martyrs and Saint Ursula with her eleven thousand virgins. The procession ends up at Barney Kiernan's pub: where else?

(443, line 6) Bloom reappears *(when be damned but in he comes again*) and Martin tells him that he is ready to go to see the late Paddy Dignam's widow. The narrator expresses the poisonous, vicious hatred that has now erupted against Bloom. He seems to be in imminent danger of violence. Bloom and Martin and the two others leave hurriedly but the citizen and the little mob from the pub follow them out, still jeering. Martin urges the driver (the jarvey) to get going but Bloom is standing up in the jaunting car telling them about famous jews including Christ. *And the Saviour was a jew and his father was a jew. Your God.*

The now infuriated citizen, grabs the biscuit box (previously used as a source of treats for the dog) and throws it at Bloom – but misses. The horse takes fright and the jaunting car is taken off at speed, with the dog chasing uselessly after them, carrying Bloom and his companions safely away.

The getaway is given an inflated and majestic description by the other narrator (445), followed by the first narrator's highly entertaining eyewitness account of the scene *(A large and appreciative gathering of friends...)* This in turn is interleaved with the other narrator's interpretations of the event as first, a grand farewell gathering and then, with the ineffective landing of the biscuit box, as a devastating geological upheaval. (447). The episode ends with a brief mock-biblical account in which Bloom is miraculously, like Elijah, raised up to heaven *like a shot off a shovel.*

Notes on Episode 13: NAUSICAA (449-499)

In Homer, Odysseus is shipwrecked and washed up on a beach where he goes to sleep.

Nausicaa, daughter of King Alcinous, comes to the beach with her two maids to wash her clothes. Their noisy ball game wakes Odysseus who introduces himself and Nausicaa leads him to her father's palace as a guest. (Her name is derived from the Greek for a ship.)

This episode is really easy to follow and comes as a respite, both for the reader and for Bloom who is having a rest on some rocks on Sandymount Strand (beach). The time is now 8 p.m.

The opening paragraph sets the scene for us: *The summer evening had begun to fold the world in its mysterious embrace.*

Nearby is the Church of Mary, Star of the Sea, from which the sounds and smells of a service of benediction are wafted to those on the strand.

Seated on the rocks are three young women. Playing on the sands nearby are the four-year-old Caffrey twins, Tommy and Jacky. They are watched over by their big sister, Cissy Caffrey. Her friend, Edy Boardman, is in charge of her little brother 'Baby' Boardman (11 months) who is in his pushcar (pram).

The third friend, Gerty MacDowell, is not encumbered with childcare duties and she will occupy most of our attention. Also paying her attention, sitting on the rocks some distance away, is Mr Bloom. It is now 8 p.m. and we have not seen him since 6 p.m. when he left Barney Kiernan's pub.

The style of this episode is a new one, a parody of the kind of romantic fiction which young women of the time might be reading in magazines or novelettes. It is sweet, cloying, knowing, full of clichés and amusing for the reader. It is also, in its portrayal of Gerty, rather touching.

To begin with, we watch Cissy and Edy trying to cope with the minor delinquencies of the twins. Gerty is only introduced when Cissy says, teasingly, *I know who is Tommy's sweetheart. Gerty is Tommy's sweetheart.*(452)

*But who was Gerty? Gerty…was in very truth as fair a specimen of winsome Irish girlhood as one could wish to see.*There follows an admiring description of Gerty's appearance (with a few asides about her more intimate personal problems). On p 454 we are offered direct access to her inner world as she broods over young Reggie Wylie who used to ride his bicycle up and down in front of her window but has now stopped. We learn more about Gerty's clothes and then her yearning for *a truly manly man* to be her husband.

Her thoughts are interrupted by a dispute among the children over possession of the ball. Cissy Caffrey says *an unladylike thing.* Edy Boardman *says she was sure the gentleman opposite heard what she said.* The gentleman is of course Mr Bloom whose background presence is mentioned for the first time.

Next (460) we hear the sounds of a service coming from the church where a men's temperance retreat is being conducted. This reminds Gerty of her father's unfortunate tendency to drunkenness and consequent domestic violence. She feels sorry for him, loves him still and hopes he won't have a stroke and die like poor Mr Dignam. She daydreams about the chivalrous young gentlemen of old, as portrayed in Christmas almanacs.

Back to the twins playing ball (462, last para). A hard kick from Master Jacky sends the ball right up to the gentleman in black. He throws it back but it ends up just under Gerty's skirt. Gerty kicks and misses. She tries again – lifting her skirt a little, aware that the gentleman is watching her. This time she succeeds; she ventures a look at Bloom *and the face that met her gaze there in the twilight, wan and strangely drawn, seemed to her the saddest she had ever seen* (463).

The church service continues; the two other girls are occupied with the children. Gerty wishes to goodness they would all go home (bottom of 464). She and Bloom continue their silent communication; Gerty wondering about his past. She begins, in spite of everything, to think that he might be her dream-husband. Listening to the continuing sounds from the church she almost believes that, like the Virgin Mary, she herself might be a refuge for sinners.

The other two girls begin to get ready to go home (469) and Cissy decided to ask the gentleman on the rocks (*my uncle Peter over there*) what the time is. *So she went over* (top of 470). But it seems his watch has stopped. Gerty's thoughts continue to swing from her romantic connection with Bloom to the priests in the church as they conduct the service. Finally, after a teasing but wounding remark from Edy *(was she heartbroken about her best boy throwing her over)* Edy and Cissy start to depart with the children.

Gerty is left with her own thoughts about the beauty of the twilight scene, her bedroom with her cherished objects, her love of romantic poetry, an accident on Dalkey hill that might have marred her beauty: and back to wondering about Bloom and whether he might be mourning a lost love.

Suddenly, little Jackie calls out to his sister and they all see that a firework display is lighting up the sky (475). They all become excited and Gerty, knowing that Bloom is still watching her, leans back so that her skirt rides up further and further, showing him her legs up to her knickers (476). Gerty is overwhelmed with erotic love (*she would fain have cried out to him chokingly, held out her snowy slender arms to him to come*…(477)

And then a rocket sprang up and bang shot blind and O! then the Roman candle burst and it was like a sigh of O! and everyone cried O! O! The fireworks have elicited ecstatic feelings in both Gerty and Bloom who, as we shall see, has had an explosion of his own.

Gerty waves her little perfume-soaked cotton wool at her 'lover', and as she turns and moves off (479, line 6), another voice says: *Tight boots! No. She's lame! O!*

We have suddenly been switched to Bloom's point of view, where we shall stay until almost the end of the episode:

Mr Bloom watched her as she limped away. Poor girl! That's why she's left on the shelf and the others did a sprint. And he muses on the strangeness (and attractiveness) of women: their excitement over clothes; their (hypocritical) fondness for their female friends; the effects of their periods. He tries to work out what Gerty can have seen in him. But, after all, didn't Molly find him attractive when they were

younger? He wonders why his watch stopped at half past four. (482) Then he thinks:
Was that just when he, she?
O, he did. Into her. She did. Done.
Ah!

4.30 pm. must have been about the time that Molly and Boylan started having sex. It's a stunning, crushing realisation for him. The act that he dreaded has been done.

He recomposes his wet shirt and begins to feel cold and clammy. His thoughts move rapidly by free association: Gerty; an encounter with a prostitute (girl in Meath Street that night, 482).

483 He sees the girls and the children in the distance watching the fireworks. Molly's first kiss, aged 15, in Gibraltar with Lieutenant Mulvey. The girls on the strand - *those lovely seaside girls* (that music-hall song that Boylan sings). He sees the girls again and Gerty appears to look round at him. Did me good, he thinks, reliving the experience. His rambling thoughts about every aspect of womankind are punctuated by feeling the wetness of his shirt against his skin. He smells Gerty's perfume in the air (488). Back to memories of Molly and her sexiness. All sorts of events of the day recur to his mind in a jumble.

490, second para: *Howth. Bailey light. Two, four, six, eight, nine*. Bloom is looking at the flashes from the lighthouse on the promontory of Howth Head which juts into the sea. It was on Howth (pronounced 'Hoath') that he and Molly had their first kisses. It is getting cold and damp. More rueful thoughts about Gerty: *O sweet little, you don't know how nice you looked.* And later: *Sad about her lame of course but must be on your guard not to feel too much pity. They take advantage.* (491).

From here on, I shall only give you a selection of the words and images that pass through Bloom's mind. You will be able to recognise many of the references and you can just pass over the rest – until your next reading of *Ulysses* when it will reveal more of itself.

Bloom's thoughts get more and more mixed up and fragmentary. He is feeling sleepy now. He remembers playing charades with Molly at a party at Dolphin's Barn (a Dublin suburb).The sight of a flying creature diverts him to birds and bats; then sailors and light house keepers and boat rides. Sweet memories of Milly as a child and thoughts of Molly's girlhood in Gibraltar.

Better not stick here all night like a limpet (496). Time to go. He has had a long day. But brief memories of events of the day continue to crowd in. He wonders if Gerty will come back tomorrow and, picking up a stick, he starts to write a message for her in the sand but gives up, realising it will only be washed away.

499. The cuckoo clock in the priest's house sounds three times. Gerty was near enough to hear it (we are told) *and she noticed at once that the foreign gentleman that was sitting on the rocks was*
   Cuckoo
   Cuckoo

Cuckoo

Or we might think that Bloom heard it as a mocking call of 'cuckold' because Boylan has been and done the deed.

Notes on Episode 14: OXEN OF THE SUN (499-561)

Time: 10 p.m. Place: The Dublin Maternity Hospital in Holles Street.

In Homer, Odysseus and his companions arrive at the Isle of the Sun. Odysseus warns his men not to kill any of the sacred Oxen of the Sun-God for food; but in the night they disobey him. This is regarded as sacrilege by the Sun-God who strikes them all dead with a thunderbolt. Only Odysseus/Ulysses is left alive.

What's the connection with Joyce's *Ulysses*? The women giving birth in the hospital are, like the sacred cattle, symbols of fertility against whom the ribald, obscene talk of the medical students and their friends is a kind of sacrilege. Only Bloom does not join in; and he is also the only one who remains sober.

What happens in the episode? Bloom comes to the hospital to enquire about Mrs Mina Purefoy who has been three days in labour. He is invited to join a party of rowdy medical students and their friends (including some already known to us), who are sitting round a table, getting drunk and talking in a disrespectful way about sex, childbirth and related matters. Stephen Dedalus is among them and Bloom becomes concerned about his welfare and the company he is keeping: He thinks about his lost son (Rudy) and sees the young man Stephen somehow taking his place.

The style. Yes! This is what makes 'Oxen', according to Joyce himself, the most difficult episode in the whole book. It is written in a succession of styles which follow the development of English prose from its early beginnings to the time of writing. Thus, after a prologue in a sort of English with a Latin construction, we get Anglo-Saxon, Middle English, Elizabethan, and various examples of seventeen, eighteen and nineteenth century grand style as represented by many distinguished authors including Pepys, Bunyan, Defoe, Sterne, Gibbon and Charles Dickens. At the same time, according to Joyce, these different styles parallel the nine month development of the human foetus.

How should we navigate our way through this complexity of tongues? I think the best plan for first-time reader is not to worry too much about identifying the writers being imitated but to follow the narrative thread as it winds its way through. In particular, stay close to Bloom and make sure you can identify him in his various stylistic disguises. I shall provide some help with this as we proceed through.

Here we go.

First line: a call to attention: *Deshil Holles Eamus.* (repeated twice).

This means: Let us go South (or turn right) to Holles. (The maternity Hospital is in Holles Street.)

This is followed by one of Joyce's most delightful passages urging 'Horhorn' (Sir Andrew Horne, the head of the maternity hospital, alias the Sun)) to send us a new-born baby. *Send us, bright one, light one,*

Horhorn, quickening and wombfruit (repeated twice). Then the arrival of the baby boy is greeted three times: *Hoopsa boyaboy, hoopsa!*

The next three paragraphs (500 - 502) are a kind of literal translation of a rather pompous piece of Latin prose which retains the Latin word order. It is extremely hard to decipher, but reduced to its essentials it says:

'Everyone knows that it's our duty to reproduce ourselves. That's why the Celts have always cultivated medicine and established maternity hospitals so that all women, regardless of their means, can be properly attended to and cherished'.

Then, as a reward, we get the lovely alliterative sentences: *Before born babe bliss had. Within womb won he worship* (502). The paragraph continues, in less elegant but quite entertaining Anglo-Saxon style, telling how the needs of the expectant mothers are 'commodiously' met.

Now, still on 502, comes our first opportunity to identify Bloom: *Some man that wayfaring was stood by housedoor at night's coming. Of Israel's folk was that man* – (and there's your clue*). Stark ruth* means 'strongly compassionate'. The sister on duty lets him in. She is Nurse Callan whom he already knows (though her name is not mentioned till much later). Bloom apologises for failing to doff his hat when they met in the street. He had failed to recognise her because *swiftseen face, hers, so young then had looked*. Nurse Callan responds with a blush! She is concerned about his black suit but he reassures her he has not been personally bereaved. He asks after Dr O'Hare and is told that *O'Hare Doctor in heaven was*, having died of stomach cancer (*belly crab*) some three years ago. They share a feeling of sadness over the premature death of Dr O'Hare.

504. So Bloom asks after Mrs Purefoy (I think you are getting the hang of this now). He wonders why Nurse Callan herself has not yet had a baby. *(Nine twelve bloodflows chiding her childlessness.)*

In the next para, *a young learning knight yclpet* (called) *Dixon* approaches. He is a young junior doctor. He and Bloom (now referred to as *the traveller Leopold)* have previously met in an Emergency department when Dr Dixon treated him for a bee sting. (*sore wounded in his breast by a spear)*. Bloom is persuaded to join the party of students gathered round a table in what appears to be a common room (505).

In the next paragraph, the scene and the laden table are described in a sort of de-familiarising language. I have discovered that this is in the style of a 14th Century travel book by someone calling himself 'John Mandeville'.

The table was evidently made from Finnish wood and its legs are carved into figures of motionless dwarves. The *vat of silver that was moved by craft to open in which lay strange fishes withouten heads* is clearly a tin of sardines. You get the idea? So Bloom sits down and is given some beer which he discreetly pours into his neighbour's glass. The section ends piously: *Thanks be to Almighty God.*

506 the sister begs them (in the style of Mallory) to *leave their wassailing* (and be more quiet), as there is a patient in labour, whom they can hear upstairs. Bloom observes that his old acquaintance, Lenehan, is among those present, though older than the students.

On 507 The company is again described. We are told that sir Leopold sat with them because of his friendship with sir Simon (Dedalus) and his son Stephen. The students start to discuss the question of when, in a difficult labour, a choice has to be made, the life of the mother or the child should be preserved. This is difficult to follow because of the medieval style. Young Madden (one of the students) quotes an actual case in which the *husband would not let* (prevent) *her death* because of a vow he had made. Stephen asks, what about the sperms, *those Godpossibled souls that we nightly impossiblise* (through contraception). They too are being wasted. But Crotthers says he would not be concerned about the fate of the sperms *if it so fortuned him to be delivered of his spleen of lustihead.* The others all laugh except Stephen and 'sir Leopold'. Stephen says, ironically, that the Catholic opposition to contraception goes against our true nature. Bloom is asked for his opinion but escapes by making a joke about the church gaining financially from both a birth and a death.

On 510 we learn that *sir Leopold was passing grave maugre* (feeling unwell) because the cries of the women in labour reminded him of *his good lady Marion* (Molly) who had given birth to their one son, Rudy, only for him to die at 11 day old. Having lost his own son, he is *grieved for young Stephen for that he lived riotously with those wastrels and murdered his goods with whores.*

But Stephen fills the cups again and delivers a sort of sermon, giving the Church's view of the mother or child question. He compares Eve with the Virgin Mary and wonders whether she knew that Jesus was really the Father as well as the Son.

On p 512 Punch Costello starts up a bawdy song, but nurse Quigley, from the door, bids them all be quiet. Costello is subjected to a barrage of Shakespearean insults by the others. Bloom gently advises them that this sort of talk is inappropriate. But the noisy drunken arguing continues with reference to a play by Beaumont and Fletcher (*The Maid's Tragedy*) with its overt sexual content. Stephen claims that the two authors shared a 'doxy' between them and declares mockingly *Greater love than this, no man hath, that a man lay down his wife for his friend.*

On 514, line 3, adultery is condemned in the style of the Authorised Version of the Bible (Deuteronomy 32) and the 'Reproaches', which are part of the Roman Catholic Good Friday liturgy in which Christ reproaches the people (The Jews?) for their ungrateful treatment of him.

A little later on, in the lower part of 515, there is *a black crack of noise in the street.* It is a thunderstorm, but Lynch warns Stephen that his blasphemies must have made God angry. Stephen defiantly says it is only that *old Nobodaddy* (his name for God) was also *in his cups* (drunk). But he is really quite frightened by the thunder and Bloom tries to calm him with a scientific explanation.

516 In the style of John Bunyan's *Pilgrim's Progress* in which everyone and every place has an allegorical name, we are told that *young Boasthard* (Stephen) and the rest of the company are not impressed by the world of *Believe-on-Me*, preferring the attractions of *this whore Bird-in-Hand* in *her grot named Two-in-the-Bush*. Note, in the last paragraph of 51, someone called Preservative provides a contraceptive sheath *(stout shield of oxengut)*.

518 *So Thursday sixteenth June*...The diary entry signals a parody of Samuel Pepys. After describing the prelude to the storm and its arrival, the narrator describes the meeting of Malachi Mulligan (Stephen's friend and tormentor) with Alec Bannon who tells him about a girl he has been seeing in Mullingar *(a skittish heifer, big of her age and beef to the heel)*. This, of course, is Leopold and Molly's 15 year old daughter Milly whom we know from Episode 4 has been working for a photographer in Mullingar. We are immediately anxious about Milly's welfare. It is raining and the two young men hurry into Horne's (hospital). The narrator describes the scene round the table; he tells us that Bloom has recently had a dream about Molly and that Mrs Purefoy is in labour with *This her ninth chick to live.*

Buck Mulligan and Alec Bannon now make their entrance (top of 525). The style is that of the essays of Addison and Steele, in the eighteenth century. Mulligan tells the company that he is setting himself up as a 'fertiliser' (for women).

528 Half way down, *Here the listener who was none other than the Scotch student...* Later we learn that his name is Crotthers. Here, he treats young Bannon to a drink. Bannon (529) says how happy he is and shows Crotthers a locket he is wearing which has a picture of his sweetheart (who, as we know, is young Milly Bloom). He rhapsodises on her beauty and then regrets that he did not have any contraceptives with him when they were together (*Would to God that foresight had remembered me to take my cloak along* – cloak being the first of a number of euphemisms for sheath) The style has now shifted to that of Lawrence Sterne, the author of *The Life and Opinions of Tristram Shandy,* with its confidential addresses to the reader, digressions and inclusion of the name 'Kitty', which was the pseudonym for one of Sterne's lady friends.

530 Last para. Nurse Callan enters and whispers to Dr Dixon. After more student ribaldry we learn (531, bottom) that Dr Dixon is needed in the ward. Costello is rude about Nurse Callan, describing her as *a monstrous fine bit of cowflesh*! And lewdly suggesting that Dixon has *rendezvoused* her. The bawdy talk about doctors and nurses goes on until Dr Dixon tells them that Mrs Purefoy has at last been delivered of a baby. He rebukes the others for their bad behaviour and leaves.

532 last para. Mr Bloom reflects on his dislike of this kind of talk by these *overgrown children.* Costello seems to him ugly and loathsome. A monstrosity. Bloom hates the way they make fun of a woman in labour. He has learned, in middle age, to control his anger, much as he dislikes listening to this crude,

offensive chatter. He tries to tell his neighbour how relieved (534) he is that Mrs Purefoy's ordeal is now over *with the fruition of her confinement since she has been in such pain through no fault of hers.* The student says it was all due to *the husband.* The boys now congratulate the aging Mr Purefoy on his potency at *being still able to knock another child out of her.* Unless, of course, it was another and younger man. Bloom wonders to himself on the inexplicably sudden change (metempsychosis) from bawdy medical student to responsible physician *by the mere acquisition of academic titles.*

535 A new and rather pompous voice now chimes in, asking sternly what right Bloom has to criticise these young men.(*But with what fitness…*)He is, after all, an alien, graciously admitted to civil rights. He is a traitor and an ingrate. His right even to be married to Molly (*violate the bedchamber of a respectable lady*) is questioned in the course of an unpleasant and clearly antisemitic piece of rhetoric.

536 After another announcement of the birth (2nd paragraph: *The news was imparted with a circumspection*) we find the company are now swapping instances (*a strife of tongues)* of all sorts of foetal malformations, complications of labour, multiple births, mythical accounts of the progeny of humans and animals and so on. This section is in the style of Gibbon.

539 *But Malachias' tale began to freeze them with horror.* Mulligan (whose first name is Malachi) tells them a story in the Gothic Horror vein of the eighteenth century. An apparition of Haines (the Englishmen from

episode one) appears and confesses to a murder, after which he comically reminds Mulligan of their meeting later on at Westland Row station.

540 *What is the age of the soul of man?* This question introduces a passage in which Bloom has retreated into himself and is remembering episodes from his childhood, his youth as a travelling salesman for his father's business, and his first sexual experience with a whore called Bridie Kelly. No child was conceived and Bloom is still without a son.

There is none now to be for Leopold, what Leopold was for Rudolph. (Bloom's father).

541 Last para. *The voices blend and fuse in clouded silence.* Bloom's reverie is becoming confused and dreamlike (suggesting De Quincy's *Confessions of a opium eater*). He is wafted over strange landscapes. He sees *a mare leading her fillyfoal;* other, more fearsome creatures appear, tramping towards the Dead Sea from which they drink. Then *the everlasting bride* appears who is both Martha and Milly, his daughter.

At the top of page 543 our attention is switched to Francis (Costello) who is reminding Stephen of their schooldays together. Stephen speaks of his poetic talents and is somewhat crushed when Vincent Lynch tells him he will need more than *a capful of light odes* to his name before that boast can become true. The talk turns to the Gold Cup race. Sceptre, a queen of a horse, has sadly lost. The word queen prompts Lynch to tell of the pleasure he had with his own queen (his girlfriend) earlier in the day. (*I wish you could have seen my queen today,* 544 line 12). He mentions that they encountered Father Conmee just after they had made love in a field. We realise that we saw them in episode 10 ('Wandering Rocks'), in the afternoon. They were the couple who emerged in some embarrassment from behind the hedge, the girl brushing away from her dress a clinging twig.

545 Mr Bloom is seen by Malachi (Mulligan) to be staring at the red triangle on a bottle of Bass's ale and says that *his soul is far away.* However, the narrator informs us, in some rather tortuous prose, that he was merely thinking of *two or three private transactions of his own.*

546 (para 2) The company is described one more time, in a grandiose nineteenth century style. Stephen now starts a discussion about how the sex of a foetus is determined which is described as if it was a report of a scientific meeting. Do males originate from the right ovary? Or is it a difference in the sperms? Or even a mixture of both? They go on to speculate about the causation of stillbirths. Lynch thinks that Nature…*has her own good and cogent reasons* (germs may have taken up residence in a seemingly healthy child); and Stephen brings the whole discussion down to a ridiculous level by suggesting that an omnivorous being (God) may like, from time to time, to eat something easily digestible such as young child or a newborn calf, known in the abattoir as *staggering bob* (550).

550 (last para) *Meanwhile the skill and patience had brought about a happy* accouchement. There is praise for Mina Purefoy and her husband Theodore (Doady) in the style of Dickens at his most sentimental.

552 *There are sins* A Cardinal Newman style paragraph reminds us how past sins can haunt a person.

3rd para. *The stranger still regarded on the face before him*...Bloom, looking at Stephen, sees an expression of *false calm.* Stephen's previous remarks seem very bitter. Bloom is reminded of an evening playing bowls *(a shaven space of lawn one May evening)*; The 4 or 5-year-old Stephen was being supported by the hands of a group of young women, while casting reproachful glances at his mother. Stephen was dressed in linsey-woolsey (a fabric made of linen and wool) which reminds Bloom of his lost son, Rudy.

553 2nd para There is another flash of lightning followed by a crash of thunder and a cloudburst.

554*Burke's! Outflings my lord Stephen*...Burke's is the public house that he calls them all to go to. Everyone rushes for the door. Bloom pauses to ask Nurse Callan to send a kind word to Mrs Purefoy and offers her a rather clumsy good wish*: Madam, when comes the storkbird for you?*

The prose remains lofty for a short while longer as Theodore Purefoy is praised. He is urged not to envy Derby and Joan who are burdened with all sorts of ailments. He should drink Mrs Purefoy's milk which *displodes in abundance.*

555(last para) The style becomes rapidly disjointed from here on and soon consists, in Joyce's words, of 'a frightful jumble of pidgin English, cockney, Irish, Bowery slang and broken doggerel'.

557 They reach the pub and drinks (including absinthe) are ordered. What we now hear is the jumble of voices shouting to be heard in the pub. Amid the linguistic chaos we can find cryptic references to previous events or conversations in the story. They include: Bloom's watch (*winding of his ticker*) Bloom's bee-sting *(Got bet by a boomblebee)* Molly's luxuriant charms (*See her in her dishabilly*). The drunken babble continues until the landlord calls *Closingtime, gents. Eh?* They spill out onto the street, still shouting.

561 *Lynch! Hey! Denzille Lane this way. Change here for Bawdyhouse.* Stephen calls Lynch to come with him to the brothel district. Someone sees, or thinks he sees an American style evangelist. *Elijah is coming washed in the Blood of the Lamb.* And the hot gospeller has the last word: *He's got a cough mixture with a punch in it for you my friend, in his backpocket. Just you try it on.*

Congratulations! You have just completed the most difficult episode in *Ulysses*. And understood as much of it as you needed.

Notes on Episode 15: CIRCE (561-703)

Time: midnight (12 a.m.) Place: The Mabbot Street entrance to 'Nighttown', the Dublin Red Light District.

In Homer, Circe, the witch, drugs an advance party of Odysseus's men and turns them into pigs. Going to investigate, Odysseus is met by the god Hermes who gives him a herb which will prevent him from being turned into a pig himself. He is able to overpower Circe and rescue his comrades. Odysseus and Circe become lovers and they all stay for a year! (This does not happen in Joyce's version.)

This episode, the longest in the book, is set entirely as a play, with the 'stage directions' in italics. The action is a mixture of dream-like visions (mainly Bloom's) and 'reality', though we switch rapidly between one mode and the other. There are appearances in the dreams (or hallucinations), by dead characters such as Bloom's father and grandfather, Stephen's mother and even the corpse of Paddy Dignam. Several inanimate objects and a few abstract ideas also have their say. So it's quite a pantomime.

Mostly, it is easy to follow if you let yourself go with the flow.

Mabbot Street is a place of poverty and squalor. It has the quality of a nightmare. The inhabitants all seem to be victims of disability, alcohol or violence. But some children are enjoying ice-creams from Rabaiotti's 'gondola'. Cissy Caffrey, who was a respectable girl when we last saw her (in Episode 13, Nausicaa) appears as a whore and sings a bawdy song (563). Two

British soldiers (Privates Carr and Compton) stumble along, followed by Stephen and Lynch. Stephen is chanting the introitus from the Latin Mass.

Stephen starts talking about a universal language consisting of gestures. He tells Lynch they are going to look for Georgina Johnson, a prostitute he remembers fondly from a previous visit.

Page 565 begins, in italics, a long section of description reminiscent of the opening fog of Dickens's *Bleak House*. Bloom eventually appears *flushed, panting and cramming bread and chocolate into a side pocket*. He disappears into a pork butcher's and emerges with two snacks: a crubeen (a pig's foot) and a sheep's trotter. Trying to cross the road, he narrowly misses being run down by a tramcar strewing sand on the track. He encounters further interruptions from a strange Spaniard, a rag-and-bone man and the two Caffrey children. He talks, or thinks to himself, in the interior monologue with which we are now familiar.

568 (4th line from bottom) Leopold's deceased father, Rudolph (*a stooped bearded figure*), now approaches. His father treats Leopold as though he was an errant teenager and scolds him for getting into bad company and wasting money. He recalls a day when young Leopold got drunk at a meeting of the Harriers running club. His mother (Ellen Bloom, née Higgins) pops up too. Then a sharp voice calls his name: *Poldy!* (570). It is his wife Molly (alias Marion) Bloom, very imperious in a Turkish costume and with a camel! Then, even the bar of soap that he pulls from his pocket

recites, or sings, a little verse (middle of 571). Anything can happen in this hallucinatory world.

Outside a brothel an *elderly bawd*, tries to sell Bloom a 15-year old *maidenhead* for ten shillings (572). Gerty MacDowell (from Nausicaa), now presented as a prostitute also, reminds him of their silent exchanges on the seashore. This brief encounter is followed by a long conversation with Mrs Breen, Molly's friend, with whom Leopold liked to flirt before they were married. In this 'dream', they reminisce and start flirting again. You will notice that everyone in this episode, especially Bloom, is liable to an instant change of clothes when a change of status or identity requires it. For example, at the top of page 577, both he and Mrs Breen have a sudden change of costume when they recall a meeting at Leopardstown races.

The now unacceptable passage about black entertainers (573) should be passed over quickly).

578. Mrs Breen *fades from his side* and the scene changes back to one of squalor in which a gang of *loiterers* are listening to a tale from their *gaffer* about someone who was taken short and emptied his bladder into a bucket in the street which unfortunately contained porter (beer) placed there by some plasterers. Bloom (of course), was the culprit.

The streets become more noisy with laughter and shouting and the obscene invitations of the whores. Bloom is searching for Stephen, whom he has followed on the train, concerned about his welfare, although not sure why. (*Wildgoose chase this.*579, last para).

On 580 there is a series of bewildering encounters, including one with that horrible dog, Garryowen from the 'Cyclops' episode, who ends up being given the crubeen and the sheep's trotter (581). Then, two members of the Watch, the Dublin civic police force, appear and they *each lay a hand on Bloom's shoulder,* repeating his name: *Bloom Of Bloom. For Bloom. Bloom (581).*

Things now slide rapidly downhill for Bloom. *Come. Name and address.* say the Watch, accusingly. Bloom says he has forgotten. He tries to defend himself by pleading that he has been doing good to animals by feeding the dog. Cruelty to animals is represented by Signor Maffee, the lion tamer from *Sweets of Sin*, the sexy book that Bloom rented for Molly, earlier in the day.

However, the questioning by the Watch is going badly despite Bloom's desperate efforts to clear himself, employing false identity claims and sly suggestions of influence in high places.

583 The situation is not helped when Martha, his secret correspondent, turns up to claim him.

Then he tries to pass himself off as an ex-soldier who has fought for King and Country. When he claims to be a journalist, he is accused of plagiarism by Philip Beaufoy, the author of the story he was reading in Photo-Bits, on the toilet this morning, which gave him the idea of writing a winning story himself (585).

Next up (586), is Mary Driscoll, formerly the Blooms servant whom Molly suspected of stealing and to whom, according to Miss Driscoll, he made improper suggestions.

587 All these accusations lead naturally to a courtroom scene in which the Clerk of the Court makes an

announcement: *Order in the Court! The accused will now make a bogus statement.* The statement is recorded in indirect speech (italics), followed by a cross-examination. Bloom's barrister, J.J. O'Molloy (the seedy, impoverished lawyer) in a wonderful display of eloquence, enters a protest: *This is no place for indecent levity at the expense of an erring mortal disguised in liquor* (bottom of p 588). And then launches on a magnificent plea of mitigation for his client.

591 Bloom attempts to give the names of some distinguished referees, but is stopped by the irruption of three society ladies who, each in turn, accuse of him of attempting to seduce them in disgusting ways. Mrs Yelverton Barry speaks first. They want to punish him with whipping. Bloom indicates that a mild stimulating 'spanking' would be fine with him. But the ladies have in mind something much more painful.

On p 595, a cuckoo clock calls three times and the 'cuckolding' of Bloom by Boylan is recalled by the jingling of the loose brass quoits on the marital bed. A panel of fog rolls back to reveal the 'jury': all friends or acquaintances of the accused. The dream now becomes even more nightmarish for Bloom as the Recorder sentences him to death (596). The corpse of Paddy Dignam does his best to confirm Bloom's alibi (he was at a funeral).

On page 599, we are, perhaps, back in the real world, but not for long. *Zoe Higgins a young whore in a sapphire slip* tells him that the person he is looking for (Stephen) is inside the brothel. She tries to interest him in having sex, but his mind is becoming engaged in ideas for social improvement.

The Chimes from a distant steeple (601) call him to *Turn again. Leopold! Lord mayor of Dublin!*

And his political career is launched. We are now in an extended dream sequence in which Leopold's rousing speech on the hustings is an astounding success. Huge crowds have come to hear him and the scale of the occasion is wonderfully exaggerated and sent up. Soon Bloom is the object of universal admiration and adoration. He is acclaimed *emperor president and king chairman... King Leopold the First!* by the Bishop of Down and Connor (604). Bloom graciously accepts and announces that *a new era is about to dawn... The new Bloomusalem* (606). His bodyguard distribute gifts to all. His powers have become magical; he does a sort of royal walkabout, greeting his people (608). He makes a speech consisting of a jumble of Hebrew words starting with the letters of the alphabet (*Aleph Beth Ghimel Daleth).* Presumably this is all the Hebrew that he remembers from early lessons from his father (609). He invites and answers questions, offers free advice and sets out his programme of reform (610).

612. However, dissenting voices are now heard and opposition starts to grow, coming to a head when the American evangelist, Alexander J Dowie, violently denounces Bloom and calls for him to be lynched. *Objects of little or no commercial value* are thrown at the great man. In desperation he calls on Dr Malachi Mulligan (yes, the same Buck Mulligan) to give medical testimony on his behalf (613). Other medical students contribute and there is an astonishing climax

in which Bloom gives birth to eight extremely talented baby boys. He follows this achievement with a further sequence of miraculous stunts culminating in causing an eclipse of the sun with his little finger. Brini, the Papal Nuncio, then appears and recites a genealogical table which shows that Bloom is a direct descendant of the biblical Moses, by way of a string of improbable ancestors. Finally he announces in Latin that '*his name is Emmanuel'*. In other words he is the Messiah. But soon people are denying that he is the true messiah. He is to be stoned and defiled and to carry the sins of the world (in which his fate is to resemble that of Jesus). The Dublin Fire Brigade (by general request) set fire to Bloom. However, he seems to emerge virtually unscathed with only traces of burning and is venerated by 'the daughters of Erin'.

619 We are back in the 'real world' and Zoe, the whore, renews her attempts to persuade Bloom to be her client. Bloom prevaricates and makes excuses about being a married man (*Somebody would be dreadfully jealous if she knew*). But he agrees to go in (nearly falling on the threshold). He thinks about *all the male brutes that have possessed her*. And, sure enough, the Male Brutes appear in various devilish manifestations.

621 In the house, Lynch is sitting cross-legged on the floor waving a poker like a wand. He is with another girl called Kitty. At the pianola stands Stephen who is playing 'empty fifths' with two fingers. (The fifth note is half way up the scale to the octave.) Stephen starts talking about musical history but soon degenerates into

nonsense and has a conversation with Lynch's cap which is lying on the floor.

623 Florry (another whore) tries to join in the erudite discussion. She tells everyone that *the last day* (end of the world) *is coming this summer.* And on 624, The End of the World makes a personal appearance and says a few flippant words.

I should warn you at this point that we have entered one of the chaotic passages in the Circe episode. You may have noticed that these alternate with sections in which one character seems to be in control of the narrative: sometimes Bloom but also others, inhabitants of his inner world.

Rather than itemise every forthcoming incident in this section I will just provide a few sign posts:

624 (last few lines), Elijah (alias the American evangelist), briefly takes charge.

625 He refers to the Almighty as The President and suggests that Zoe and Florry have *got religion way inside them.* All three girls make excuses for their fall from grace.

Various characters from previous episodes of Ulysses make appearances, followed by

Mananaan Maclir, a sea god from Irish mythology.

628 Lynch tosses Zoe a cigarette and lifts the hem of her slip with his poker.

Then, in an italic passage, there is a dramatic entrance, down the chimney chute by Lipoti Virag who is

Leopold Bloom's grandfather! (The family name was originally Virag which is Hungarian for 'flower'. Bloom's father anglicised it to 'Bloom'.) Grandfather now takes charge for the next eight pages.

He proceeds to appraise and evaluate the three whores for his grandson's benefit. He notes their physical shortcomings. He has some medical knowledge and suggests a few remedies. He and Bloom go on to discuss female sexuality and vulnerability of women to rodents and serpents. (633)

Virag starts to worry about a moth which is persistently flying onto the light shade and he starts to identify with the creature *(I fear he shall be most badly burned)*.

634 Bloom's alter ego Henry Flower enters; Stephen muses to himself;

635 The Siamese twins, Philip Drunk and Philip Sober (Oxford dons with lawnmowers) make a contribution. Zoe speaks of a priest who *came to do his bit of business with his coat buttoned up.* Virag says to hell with the pope and descends into obscenity (636). His next interjection puts arguments challenging the divinity of Jesus with several different alternative explanations.

637. Virag becomes increasingly incoherent and appears to be having an epileptic fit. Ben Dollard ('the barreltone' from the episode in the Ormond Hotel), makes an appearance.

638 Virag is rapidly degenerating in appearance. He says farewell and bizarrely exits carrying his own

head. Florry thinks Stephen is a spoiled priest. He obligingly turns into a Cardinal and is persecuted by a cloud of midges.

640 Bloom offers chocolate to everybody and Zoe hands it round.

THEN:

641 *The door opens. Bella Cohen, a massive whoremistress enters.* This formidable person, Bloom's dream nemesis, is the Madame of the brothel and the ringmaster of Bloom's latent masochistic secret fantasies. In Homeric terms, she is Circe the Witch. She takes charge of the narrative until p 655.

642 Bloom has a flirtatious conversation with Bella's fan.

643 The fan orders him to kneel at Bella's feet and fasten the bootlace on her 'hoof'. His inner submissiveness rejoices as he happily complies. Bella then orders him down on all fours. She changes into a man (now called 'Bello'), while Bloom's latent femininity is released. He has become (for the duration of the fantasy), a woman.

644 Bello threatens Bloom with dire punishments. He sits on 'her' face while the whores, assisted by the cook, hold 'her' down. He quenches his cigar angrily on her (Bloom's) ear. Further humiliation and feminisation of Bloom follow. The text is easy to follow!

649 Bloom confesses to a liking for wearing female clothes and passing urine sitting down. Bello says he must do it standing. *The sins of the past are rising against you,* he says. And the Sins of the Past, duly appear, accusing Bloom *in a medley of voices.*

650 Bello demands more confessions. *Something to amuse me.* He issues a detailed list of Bloom's domestic and sexual duties as his slave. He makes it clear that she (Bloom) is to become one of the whores in his establishment. Her finer points are demonstrated, as if she were a cow, and she is sold by auction to the highest bidder (the Caliph Haroun Al Raschid)).

652 Bello continues to humiliate and embarrass Bloom. He mocks Bloom's lack of virility and tells him that *a man of brawn* (Boylan) *is in possession there* (Bloom and Molly's bedroom). Bloom, distraught, calls to Molly for forgiveness but it is his daughter, Milly, who appears (with her lover) and cries *My! It's papli! But. O Papli, how old you've grown!*

654 Bello continues to torment Bloom, finally telling her to sign her will and die; she is reduced to tearless weeping (655). *Dark shawled figures of the circumcised* mourn his fate: their names are those of old Jewish friends, referred to but not appearing in the text. He appears to have died on a funeral pyre. But then – *out of her oak frame a nymph with hair unbound…descends from her grotto and passing under interlacing yews, stands over Bloom.* She is the portrait of a nymph which hangs over the head of Leopold and Molly's bedroom. Bloom, restored to life, crawls out of the shrubbery.

The nymph reminds Bloom how he found her *in evil company*. He discovered her picture in a magazine called 'Photo-Bits', cut it out and then *bore me away, framed me in oak and tinsel and set me above the marriage couch.* Bloom and the nymph have a conversation in which he apologises for the suffering (and defacing) she had endure, trapped inside his and Molly's bedroom. The mention of a leaky chamber pot brings in The Waterfall, whose sound is *Poulaphouca* (the name of well-known waterfall not far from Dublin). The chorus of yew trees remind Bloom of a high school excursion to Poulaphouca. They were 'Halcyon Days' full of unfulfilled sexual excitement, culminating on this occasion in a secret masturbation, aroused by the sight of flaxen-haired Lottie Clarke rolling downhill (659). There is a brief intercut of Howth Hill with a dummy version of Bloom rolling, *rotatingly from the Lion's Head cliff into the purple waiting waters.* The nymph now tells him that *we immortals* have no vagina or pubic hair (as he saw earlier when inspecting the marble goddesses in the National Museum). She seems to have turned into one of these classical sculptures and Bloom apologises for the scenes she has been forced to witness from the picture frame in his bedroom. Other voices suggest that human buttocks are not at all cold. The waterfall is heard again and the nymph, now *eyeless in a nun's white habit* calms down and speaks of convents and shrines.

Bloom gets up and the back button of his trousers suddenly pops off with a Bip! (half-way down 661). Two sluts sing a bawdy little song (*O Leopold lost the pin of his drawers*) but he tells them *You have broken the spell.*

The Bip! of the exploding button has signalled the recovery of his masculinity and his self-confidence.

662 The nymph now becomes outraged and accuses him of attempting her virtue as a large moist stain appears on her robe. She threatens his genitals with a poniard (dagger). Bloom recovers his self-esteem, seizes her hand and pours scorn on her human weakness. In shame, she flees.

And is replaced by Bella, who is now female again. Bloom, having returned to his normal maleness, is no longer submissive and not at all afraid of her. They trade insults until Bella's concern for her piano returns us, for a while, to the reality of an ordinary brothel.

(663) Zoe and the other girls come back, accompanied by Stephen and Lynch. Bloom asks Zoe to return his lucky potato.

664 Bella, still worried about the piano asks *Who's paying here*? Stephen keeps putting more money on the table. There is a dispute about how much is owing and Bloom, now calmly in charge, reclaims Stephen's overpayment and offers to take care of his money for him.

666 (middle) Stephen is wondering what has happened to his former prostitute lover, Georgina Johnson. Zoe tells him *It was a commercial traveller married her and took her away with him.* Bloom tries to discourage Stephen from smoking. He is trying to take care of him.

667 *Any boy want flogging?* Father Dolan, who has just popped up, is a fearsome master from Stephen's old school, Clongowes Wood Academy (described in Joyce's earlier book, *Portrait of the Artist as a Young Man)*. The more kindly Don John Conmee had saved him from punishment with the 'pandybat'.

668 The conversation continues. Zoe reads the palms of Bloom and Stephen.

669-70 Suddenly, a hackney car (horse-drawn of course), turns up with Lenehan and Blazes Boylan aboard. Boylan crows about his conquest of Molly. Bloom becomes his accomplice, and is invited to witness their sex act. This sounds frightful, but Bloom seems to derive a voyeuristic pleasure from the experience.

671 Bloom and Stephen both look into a mirror and see the face of Shakespeare who comments: *Tis the loud laugh bespeaks the vacant mind.*

Appearances by Paddy Dignam's widow and Mr and Mrs Martin Cunningham follow.

672-4 At Zoe's request, Stephen now gives a florid description of the delights of Paris – in English with a sort of French style diction and word order. (*Thousand places of entertainment to expenses your evening…*)

674-5 He gives a hunting cry *Hola! Hillyho!* which is answered by his father, Simon Dedalus. The scene dissolves into a noisy foxhunt which turns into a horse race with bookies crying the odds and even a commentary on the race.

676 The two soldiers (Privates Carr and Compton), with Cissy Caffrey, pass outside the window singing 'My Girl's a Yorkshire Girl'. Zoe calls for a dance and puts two pennies in the pianola; Stephen dances with Zoe; and Professor Maginni (the dancing teacher) gives a solo performance. Other characters appear and the dancing becomes general until Stephen says *Dance of death*. His dead mother rises *stark through the floor*. (Bottom of 680)

Buck Mulligan appears on cue to remind Stephen that *She's beastly dead* (681)

The mother movingly responds: *I was once the beautiful May Goulding. I am dead.*

Stephen is again put through agonies of guilt about his mother's death. She calls on him to repent or *face the fires of hell*. He continues to reject her and her religion, becomes hysterical (683) and, lifting his ashplant (stick), he smashes the chandelier with a cry of *Nothung!* (This is the name of Siegfried's miraculous sword in Norse mythology and Wagner's Ring cycle.)

There is pandemonium with Bella calling for the police; Stephen rushes out, along with Lynch.

Bella asks who is to pay for the lamp and demands ten shillings. Bloom again takes charge with impressive gravity. Pointing out that the damage is slight, he throws a shilling on the floor.

At the bottom of 684 there begins a long passage in italics. Bloom hurries out and *from the left arrives a jingling hackney car*. The passengers are Corny

Kelleher (the funeral director) and *two silent lechers*. Bloom, trying to disguise himself with a hood, hurries out down the steps. A pack of bloodhounds picks up his scent and he is pursued by a noisy mob who pelt him with rubbish. The crowd includes a large number of minor characters from *Ulysses*, featuring in many different episodes. Like all Joyce's lists, it will reveal, if read carefully, a number of comic surprises.

Back in the street (686) Bloom catches up with Stephen who has become involved in a stand-off with the two Privates who accuse him of insulting first, Cissy Caffrey, and then King Edward VII! One soldier encourages the other to violence while Stephen, careless of the danger, remains aloof and provocative.

688 Bloom elbows his way through the crowd and takes charge again, calling Stephen 'Professor'. Private Carr goes on about the insults to the King, who now appears in person and shakes everyone by the hand. Bloom tries to pacify the soldiers and get Stephen to Safety (690). The dream world enfolds the scene again and a variety of characters featured in previous episodes re-appear. They include 'the citizen' (episode 12, The Cyclops), the Croppy Boy, tragic hero of the song performed in the Ormond Hotel by Ben Dollard (11, The Sirens), and Rumbold, the Demon Barber and hangman (also from 12). The Croppy Boy is hanged with gruesomely humorous results and a reappearance of the three fashionable ladies who tormented Bloom earlier in the present chapter. The quarrelsome soldiers resume their threats to beat up Stephen. In the confusion, Voices call for the Police again and there are shouts of *Dublin's burning!* (694).

There is a further long passage of italic description, inflating and parodying the scene with more guest appearances.

696 We are back to reality with one of the soldiers (Private Carr) threatening Stephen with violence. Finally, inevitably (697), Private Carr punches Stephen in the face, knocking him to the ground.

Two members of The Watch now appear and one asks *What's wrong here?*

Bloom tries to enlist their sympathy but they remain officious. Happily, Corny Kelleher then (the funeral director), *appears among the bystanders* (698) and Bloom whispers to him that the fallen man is the son of Simon Dedalus, a well-known and respected citizen. Kelleher uses his authority and between them they persuade the Watch that *Boys will be boys* and that Stephen's involvement in the brawl was just a foolish student escapade. They had all been the same at his age. The Watch move off. And Bloom and Kelleher tell each other that neither had any intention of entering the brothel. The horse gives a loud neighing laugh in disbelief. Kelleher gets back in the car and the jarvey (driver) carries him off. Bloom wakes Stephen who is incoherently reciting fragments of poetry. Bloom, standing guard over him, is reminded of the face of Stephen's mother.

Finally (702-703) Mr Bloom has a very touching vision of his own son, Rudy – as the eleven-year-old boy he might have become, had he lived.

PART III

Notes on Episode 16: EUMAEUS (704 -776)

Time: 1 a.m. Place: The cabmen's shelter, Butt Bridge.

In Homer, Odysseus finally makes his way back to Ithaca, his home, disguised as a beggar. He goes to the hut of his faithful old swineherd, Eumaeus, who fails to recognise his master. He later reveals himself to his son, Telemachus. Father and son have a joyful reunion and plan to destroy Penelope's suitors.

The style The story is now taken over by a narrator. He seems to have a limited literary ability but is trying hard to impress, avoiding simple words in favour of posh alternatives. His style, anything but straightforward, is packed with circumlocutions, clichés and hilariously inappropriate similes. His sentences at first sight look long and tedious. But don't be deceived into skimming quickly through the verbiage. Joyce's apparently clumsy, careless writing is actually very cleverly done. If you just go with the slowly meandering rhythm, you will find it very clear and entertaining.

Preparatory to anything else Mr Bloom brushed off the greater bulk of the shavings. (I am unable to explain where these shavings came from! Perhaps you can help me?)

Bloom and Stephen have left the brothel area and are walking towards the cabmens' shelter where Bloom hopes he will be able to get Stephen a (non-alcoholic) drink. They can't find a cab and their journey on foot is painstakingly described. Note that this narrator is unable to simply say 'it had been raining' but has to describe a recent shower as *a visitation by Jupiter Pluvius.* N.B. Fidus Acchates (faithful friend).

706 2nd para. Bloom tries to give his younger companion some parental advice about the dangers of getting drunk and consorting with *women of ill fame.* Furthermore, policemen are not to be trusted and only the *providential* appearance of Corny Kelleher had saved Stephen from suffering further injury in the brothel area. Bloom adds further warnings about immoderate drinking *never beyond a certain point* and notes that Stephen's pub-hunting friends, the medicos, had all deserted him, save Lynch. *And that one a Judas* (707) says Stephen.

708 After avoiding the night watchman, Gumley, who is a friend of his father's, Stephen is saluted by another acquaintance, who turns out to be 'Long John' Corley a rather pathetic young man who is drunk and without enough money for a night's lodgings. There is a passage of direct speech between the two of them before the narrator takes over again. Meanwhile (bottom of 711) Bloom is dodging about near the watchman's brazier, waiting for Stephen and Corley to finish and part.

713 Having heard of Corley's plight, Bloom then asks Stephen where *he* is planning to sleep. Why did he leave his father's house? *To seek misfortune, was Stephen's answer.* Bloom thinks that returning to the Martello tower is a bad idea (back into bad company), and Stephen thinks about the sad, impoverished life of his younger sisters at home. Bloom again warns

against the malign influence of Mulligan, who is simply picking Stephen's brains (715).

Bottom of 715: They reach the cabmen's shelter presided over by the 'keeper' rumoured to be the *once-famous Skin-the-Goat Fitzharris*, a member of an Irish patriot gang called 'the invincibles' who were responsible for the Phoenix Park Murders. Bloom orders a cup of rather revolting coffee and a roll for Stephen and they discuss language and names (having heard some Italians quarrelling) until a red-bearded, drunken man, probably a sailor, accosts Stephen, asking for his name. The sailor says he knows a Simon Dedalus who was a sharpshooter. This is clearly not Stephen's father. The sailor starts telling them other tales of his adventures and his listeners increasingly feel that he is making a lot of it up. One of the jarvies (cabbies) asks him if he has seen some queer sights and he obliges them with tales of cannibals in South America.

Bloom goes into a reverie about his own unfulfilled plans to travel all over Ireland and England and this merges with another favourite fantasy in which he organises a prestigious English concert tour for Molly (723). Or, maybe he could open up some new travel routes, so that *the average man* could afford to go and see the sights of England and Ireland (724).

725 The sailor starts again, trying to impress Bloom and Stephen with his stories.

726 Bloom asks Murphy (the sailor) if he has ever been to Gibraltar (where Molly was brought up). Murphy is vague and evasive. *I'm tired of all them rocks in the sea.*

So Bloom starts thinking aimlessly (*woolgathering*) about the vastness of the sea and why people feel a need to sail over it.

729 Murphy starts to show off his tattoos.

730 *The face of a streetwalker...peered round the door of the shelter.* Embarrassed, Bloom recognises her as a mentally unwell old woman who once asked if she could do the Blooms' washing for them. He finds her disgusting (though pitiable) and wonders to Stephen how she *can be barefaced enough to solicit* in her condition. Stephen says *she is a bad merchant. She buys dear and sells cheap.* Bloom renews his exploration of Stephen's views by asking him if *You, as a good Catholic...believe in the soul.* This leads to an exchange of beliefs on the existence of a supernatural God in view of the rational explanations provided by modern science.

733 Stephen ironically says this (God's existence), *has been proved conclusively by several of the best known passages in Holy Writ apart from circumstantial evidence.* Bloom concludes that on this point they will have to agree to differ. He tries to encourage Stephen to sample the unappealing coffee and bun.

735 Bloom starts taking stock of Murphy the sailor, wondering about his possibly unsavoury past and how much of what he said might be true. The possible tendency of Italians to stab people in the back leads him on to Spaniards who also have passionate temperaments; this enables him to move smoothly on to his favourite subject, Molly, who is half Spanish.

But the others start talking about ships and shipwrecks (738), until Murphy gets up and says *Let me cross your bows, mate...* He appears to be going to the toilet but they soon see and hear him urinating in the street.

There follows (in Bloom's mind) a reflection on the social downfall of the watchman, Gumley (if it is he), and then we hear some more talk about shipwrecks.

741 Skin-the-Goat, the keeper of the Shelter, starts to complain about the way Ireland's rich natural resources are being drained out of her by England. He predicts England's imminent fall from power. The sailor aggressively defends the Irish catholic peasant as *the backbone of our empire.* To which the Keeper retorts that *he cared nothing for any empire, ours or his, and considered no Irishman worth of his salt that served it.*

This prompts Bloom (743), to ruminate at length on the past history of Skin-the-Goat Fitzharris, the ex-member of a revolutionary terrorist group – if that is really who the keeper is. Bloom *confesses to himself that he feels some admiration for a man who had actually brandished a knife, cold steel, with the courage of his political convictions*: until he recollects that Skin-the-Goat was only the driver for the gang.

745 Bloom tells Stephen about his confrontation with the citizen in the Pub. Bloom emphasises his distaste for any kind of violence. In a whisper for Stephen's ear only, he describes (746), how the jews *are accused of ruining. Not a vestige of truth in it I can safely say.* Bloom would advocate *everyone having a comfortable, tidy sized income...something in the*

neighbourhood of £300 per annum. Provided they work.

Count me out says Stephen (747). But Bloom assures him that literary labour is equally important to Ireland. *Both the brain and the brawn* (748). Stephen says that Ireland is important because it belongs to him. Bloom is disconcerted by this solipsism and is led to ponder at length (748-751) how brilliant young men and even members of High Society may go off the rails. He has already spent quite a sum of money on Stephen: but still, *to cultivate the acquaintance of someone of no uncommon calibre who could provide food for reflection would amply repay any small...*

He turns his attention to the newspaper where he reads Hynes's report of the Dignam funeral. He is annoyed to find his name misspelt as 'L Boom'. Stephen reads Mr Deasy's foot-and-mouth disease letter while Bloom (or Boom) whiles away the time by reading the racing news with its account of the victory of *Throwaway.*

753 A cabman remarks that one day they will open a newspaper and find that Parnell has returned. Dubliners in *Ulysses* love to muse and speculate about their 'lost leader' who died of natural causes, shortly after the disgrace of being found in an adulterous relationship with a married woman (Kitty O'Shea). Bloom remembers, an occasion when he was able to pick up and return the great man's hat to him, after it had been knocked off in a crowded meeting. Bloom now recalls and describes to Stephen, the details of Parnell's downfall. He tells Stephen that Kitty O'Shea was a woman of hot-blooded passion, also Spanish or half so (like his own Molly).

And on p 758, he can't resist producing a faded old photograph of Molly (in her prime) which with modest pride he shows to Stephen. His satisfaction at being married to Molly is momentarily disturbed by the thought: *Suppose she was gone when he?...* But the thought of the familiar domestic disorder of their bedroom in the morning reassures him (759, last two lines).

760 His thoughts turn back to Parnell and his unfortunate entanglement; we are given a more detailed account of Bloom's brief encounter with Greatness and the return of Parnell's hat, graciously received. There are clear parallels with Molly and her alleged affairs (liaisons *between still attractive married women getting for fair and forty and younger men* (763, top).

Returning to Stephen, Bloom feels regret that the young man is wasting his time on *profligate women* and is concerned, like a parent, that the young man has had nothing to eat for more than 24 hours.

765 *It was high time to be retiring* and Bloom is wondering if he should invite Stephen to come home with him and stay the night. What would Molly think? How will Stephen receive the invitation? In the end he simply invites Stephen to come with him and talk things over. Stephen does not dissent, but seems reluctant to move and we listen to more desultory conversation from the other occupants of the shelter.

768 Eventually (*To cut a long story short*) Bloom pays the bill and they leave the shelter, Bloom supporting the still unsteady Stephen.

770 They talk amicably about music although their tastes differ a good deal. They pass a nice old horse dragging a road sweeping brush. *He was just a big foolish, noodly kind of a horse, without a second care in the world* (772). Stephen continues to talk about early music and sings a few lines, impressing Bloom with his beautiful tenor voice. His face is like his mother's but his vocal talent comes from his father. Perhaps, Bloom thinks, he could become Stephen's manager and promoter in a career as a musician. Stephen needs to be freed from the unhealthy influence of Mulligan to achieve this, however.

At this point, the horse, perhaps expressing his scepticism about Bloom's plans, slowly produces *three smoking globes of turds*.

They have reached Lower Gardiner Street and are now within a few minutes of the Blooms' home at no. 7, Eccles Street.

Notes on Episode 17: ITHACA Part 1 (776-819)
(I have divided this long episode into two parts)

In Homer's Odyssey *the corresponding chapter deals with Odysseus's return to his palace in his homeland of Ithaca where his wife Penelope is being besieged by 20 eager suitors who think her husband is dead. Odysseus eventually kills all the suitors and is reunited with Penelope.*

Again, we have completely new *style*. This episode consists entirely of questions, posed to the reader and answered by the narrator, often at some length with rigorously detailed descriptions and long words of Latin derivation. Joyce (and Stephen), are both familiar with this kind of question-and-answer formula from the *catechism* they learned in their Jesuit school education.

There is a good deal of humour in this episode although you may find that the long 'scientific' explanations threaten your patience (and your sanity).

776-8 The journey of Bloom and Stephen to Bloom's house at No. 7 Eccles Street is described. *Of what did the diumvirate deliberate during their itinerary?* Their conversation is summarised and the points on which their views diverged are noted. Bloom recalls similar rambling conversations with others.

779 They arrive at the door and Bloom can't find his latchkey. The reason for this and his solution to the problem of how to get in are carefully and comically described. The entry process and the lighting of a

candle by Bloom are then seen from Stephen's point of view.

Stephen is admitted through the front door and conducted into the downstairs kitchen where Bloom lays and lights a fire, while Stephen remembers previous fires that have been kindled for him (780-82).

The kettle is then filled and boiled. If you have ever wondered how the water gets from the reservoir into the kettle and what happens in the boiling process you will now be told; and you might be moved to protest: too much information! But you might also admire the way Joyce tells the story. We are also treated to a recital of all the many aspects of water that evoke Leopold's admiration (783-4).

Stephen, who does not like water, declines an opportunity to wash his hands.

786 Bloom thinks about, but does not give Stephen, various items of health advice.

The boiling of water is then explained and there is a brief interpolation on the advantages of shaving at night.

On p788 we have an inventory of the contents of the kitchen dresser. There will be further lists in this episode, all contributing to a rich account of life in the Bloom household.

789 The torn up betting slips must have been discarded by Boylan after he backed the wrong horse in the Gold Cup. In the Lotus Eaters episode (no.5), Bloom, by using the words 'throw away', gave Bantam Lyons the idea that he was tipping a horse called 'Throwaway' to win: which it did). He was not able to back the horse

himself but had *sustained no positive loss and brought a positive gain to others. Light to the gentiles.*

Now that the kettle has boiled, Bloom prepares cocoa for himself and his guest. Stephen drinks more slowly making Bloom think that he must be *engaged in mental composition.* He himself has tried to find the answers to certain problems in life from the works of Shakespeare: without much success. He remembers his own modest literary efforts and goes over the reasons for his failure to compose a topical song (793).

In the next section (794 - 800), he considers the relationship between Stephen and himself. He performs numerical manipulations of their respective ages; and remembers the occasions of their previous meetings. The two compare their recollections of a Mrs Riordan at different periods of her life.

Bloom regrets that he is no longer young and athletic like Stephen.

He wonders what Stephen thinks about their relationship. In what follows, it is not always clear, when the two are comparing notes and when we are just hearing Bloom's silent thoughts.

Did either openly allude to their racial differences? Neither.

Their parentages are compared and their experiences of baptism. Their difference in temperament and education are noted. Bloom notes that Stephen represents the artistic temperament and Bloom the scientific: but Bloom's tendency is towards applied rather than pure science. He muses over his ideas for possible inventions, financial schemes and the infinite possibilities, hitherto unexploited, of the modern art of advertisement.

Note the reference to the advertisement for Plumtree's Potted Meat and its suggestive slogan:
What is home without Plumtree's Potted Meat?
Incomplete.
With it an abode of bliss.

We shall find, in the last chapter, that Molly and her lover have taken some of the Plumtree product to bed with them as a snack.

801-2 Stephen sketches a romantic scene set in a hotel. This reminds Bloom painfully of the the Queens Hotel, Ennis, where his father committed suicide. But instead of telling this to Stephen, he prefers to think about the possibilities of turning Stephen's literary and narrative powers to practical and profitable use.

802 (bottom) Bloom now considers the question: *what to do with our wives?* He concludes that for Molly the best thing would be to offer her *courses of evening instruction specially designed to render liberal instructions agreeable.*

He recalls many instances of her *deficient mental development* and the attempts he has already made to improve her education.

805 Bloom informs Stephen of three historical Jewish seekers of the pure truth (all named Moses). Stephen adds Aristotle as an eminent gentile truth-seeker and Bloom says that he had been *the pupil of a rabbinical philosopher, name uncertain.*

806-7 They compare fragments of verse in ancient Hebrew and Irish: and speculate together what points of contact there might have been between the two languages.

The Jewish and the Irish peoples seem to have many things in common, including their dispersal, persecution and the possibility of national revival. (See John F Taylor's speech quoted in the newspaper office episode 7, Aeolus).

808-10 Stephen sings to Bloom an old ballad with an antisemitic theme about Little Harry Hughes and the jew's daughter. Joyce even supplies the musical notation. Bloom is quite happy with the first verse (Harry drives his ball over the jew's garden wall and smashes a window (809). The second part of the ballad introduces the jew's daughter all dressed in green, who leads him into the house where she cuts off his head with her penknife!

How did the father of Millicent receive this second part? With mixed feelings. Unsmiling,
he heard with wonder a jew's daughter, all dressed in green.

Mr Bloom is unsettled and broods about possible causes of ritual murder. Could it be done while sleepwalking? He has been a somnambulist himself and Milly used to have night-terrors. He remembers episodes from her childhood and adolescence (811-14).

814, 3rd paragraph: *What proposal…* Bloom invites Stephen to stay the night. This might have advantages for everyone. Molly could learn correct Italian pronunciation and there might be *a reconciliatory union between a schoolfellow and a jew's daughter.* (815)

Stephen declines the proposal of a night's lodging. However, he will consider another proposal: mutual instruction for Stephen and Molly in, respectively, singing and Italian. On reflection, Bloom is saddened because, although he is full of schemes to improve human life, there seem to so many obstacles to progress in the form of the *generic conditions imposed by natural, as distinct from human law, as integral parts of the human whole (*817).

818 The two men now prepare for Stephen's departure. They go into the garden, where they see, in Joyce's wonderful phrase:
   The heaventree of stars hung with humid nightblue fruit.

(Part two continues directly from where we left off on 819.)

Notes on Episode 17A: ITHACA, Part Two (819 - 871)

In the garden, Bloom demonstrates the constellations and then embarks on a series of meditations on the impossibility of calculating the vastness of the universe or the infinite smallness of the particles making it up. He is saved from attempting such calculations by the realisation that an infinite number of sheets of paper would be required to set it all down! He goes on to brood on the unlikelihood of human beings being able to live on other planets. And even if they did, their human flaws would preclude the possibility of their moral redemption (820-821).

Next, he considers the various features of the constellations and their possible celestial influences on human affairs, such as a star appearing at the time of birth or death of certain individuals. The narrator poses and answers weightily, a number of other questions about Mr Bloom's beliefs of which the last, and most entertaining is *the special affinities which appeared to exist between the moon and woman?* (823-4).

Bloom and Stephen observe the light of a paraffin lamp in a bedroom window, indicating the presence of Molly in the house and giving Bloom the opportunity to sing his wife's praises. They both need to urinate and they do so in the garden, side by side (825). Their streams are compared as are their thoughts during the process. And a shooting star marks the auspicious event!

826 Bloom lets Stephen out through the garden gate which Bloom unlocks for him. As they part they hear the bells of the church of St George.

827 Bloom reflects on the current locations of the company he travelled with to the funeral. He is reminded also of a number of companions, now deceased.

828 He decides not to wait up to see the sunrise and goes back inside the house. He bangs his head (*the right temporal lobe of the hollow sphere of his cranium*), on the angle of a walnut sideboard in the front room and realises that the furniture has been rearranged (by Molly and Boylan).

There follow detailed descriptions of the chairs and sideboard; and the piano, on which are to be found various objects left over from the adulterous pair's activities. (Smoking and singing). He burns some incense to get rid of the smells. More annotations of bric-a-brac. He looks in the mirror at his own image and sees, also, the reflection of the untidily arranged books on his shelves. The books are now individually listed and briefly or substantially described. It is as if we are visitors to the house, curiously inspecting our host's library which provides a sort of biography of the owner (832-834).

835 Mr Bloom makes himself more comfortable, by removing his collar and tie and undoing all his buttons (except for the missing trouser button which ping'd off in Bella Cohen's brothel). He is now able to scratch the scar from the old bee sting and some other places. Finding a shilling in a waistcoat pocket leads him to *compile the budget for 16 June 1904* (836). This amounts to a financial recapitulation of many events

from the day, which readers will be pleased to be able to recognise.

837 After removing his shoes and socks and attending to his toe nails, Leopold then embarks on an extended review of his *ultimate ambition* in which *all concurrent and consecutive ambitions now coalesced.* (837-847). This will be very ambitious indeed, consisting of the purchase of an ideal home (*a thatched bungalow shaped 2 storey dwelling house of southerly aspect).* The external and internal features and fittings of the house are described in amazing detail. Next comes an account of the grounds and their horticultural and sporting facilities; the possible subsequent improvements and transport facilities. This dream-house and its extensive grounds (*Bloom Cottage. Saint Leopold's. Flowerville*), have clearly been in his thoughts for a long time, with more and more details being added.

841-2 He imagines himself casually dressed, tending to the garden and enjoying other, lighter, recreations. He conjures an unstoppable rise in the social scale to the highest level, once installed. As an M.P., Privy Counsellor and justice of the peace he will uphold the law strictly but fairly. He produces anecdotal evidence *that he had loved rectitude from his earliest years* and supported progressive ideas.

844 *How much and how did he propose to pay for this country residence?* To our surprise, he has worked out a sensible and practical scheme for a mortgage, with the help of some capital in the form of gilt-edged securities, presumably inherited from his father. On the

other hand, he also has fantasies of becoming suddenly rich enough to pay for it all upfront as a result of dreaming up ingenious and profitable inventions or lucky discoveries of valuable objects (844-5). The series ends in breaking the bank at Monte Carlo and a solution of *the problem of the quadrature* (squaring*) of the circle, government premium £1,000,000 sterling.*

What else? He might produce all sorts of industrial and infrastructure improvements which would generate personal wealth (846-7).

In justification (top of 848), he notes that these extravagant daydreams *when practised habitually before retiring for the night alleviated fatigue and produced as a result sound repose and renovated vitality.*

A good night's sleep will prevent realisation of his fears of committing homicide or suicide during sleep. His final meditation is the dream of creating the perfect advertisement.

There is now a rather abrupt change of the narrator's line of questioning (last para, p848). *What did the first drawer unlocked contain?* We are going to explore the contents of two locked drawers, presumably in the sideboard, which will reveal more details of Leopold's life, in the form of letters, documents, souvenirs and guilty preoccupations.

The first drawer contains a number of old letters some from Milly, whose pet name for her father, as we kow, is 'Papli'. There is also a cameo brooch, property of Ellen Bloom, née Higgins, who was Leopold's mother. And there are the first three letters received from his clandestine female correspondent 'Martha

Clifford'; to which he will add the fourth letter which we were able to read with him in episode 5 (Lotus-eaters).

852 The second locked drawer contains his birth certificate, financial documents relating to his modestly substantial reserves; and a number of objects relating to his father Rudolph Bloom (born Virag). Reviewing the old man's possessions and his final letter (suicide note), to his son, evokes sad memories of the old man and his weaknesses. And a little remorse about his disrespect for his father's lingering Judaism.

855 Bloom is offered *partial consolation for these reminiscences* by the endowment policy and other evidence of his solvency. He muses on the dire consequences of poverty from which these assets have protected him. However, he still has a fear of being reduced to abject poverty and its miserable consequences. This could be escaped by either decease or departure to another place. He would choose the latter, and this leads to consideration of all the places in Ireland or abroad that he might translocate to; how he would get there; what sort of public notice might be displayed of his disappearance; the compulsion somehow to reappear even from the *extreme boundary of space* (856-8).

However, it is too late now for immediate departure and his thoughts turn to the comforts of sharing his wife's bed. *What advantages were possessed by an occupied, as distinct from an unoccupied bed?* (859).

Before entering the bedroom, he goes through the events of the day, giving each an Old Testament or Jewish festival label in brackets.

He ponders two enigmas.

860 On his way to the bedroom, he lists *the imperfections in a perfect day* (last para).

In the bedroom now, he sees Molly's face and is reminded of her father's. He perceives (and lists (861 *What miscellaneous effects*), the items of Molly's clothing lying on the top of her father's old trunk.

862 He observes other (impersonal), objects. He undresses and joins her in the bed, placing a pillow for his head at the foot end.

In the bed he encounters evidence of Boylan's recent presence, including the imprint of his body and some flakes of potted meat (Plumtree's, without a doubt.)

Then he reflects (863) that Boylan is only the latest of a long series of her suitors, each of whom will have imagined himself the first and only. It is not clear whether or not we are to believe that she has slept with all of them. Evidence from Molly, herself, in the final episode, will confirm our suspicion that mostly they just made a pass at her.

864 He analyses his antagonistic sentiments towards Boylan. He notes feelings of envy and jealousy and also various reasons for abnegation (setting aside the negative feelings). He lists a number of reasons why he is able to do this with *equanimity*. He decides against retribution: Boylan's actions had been natural and inevitable; and far less serious than a planetary

collision or any number of criminal activities. In any case, all possible acts of retribution are out of the question.

866 (*By what reflections,* para 3).The 'narrator' then uses his lofty, obscure style to expand on the inevitability of Molly and Boylan's adultery. The account starts with human biology and ends up with a sort of metaphor about grammatical terms. This style is often employed here by Joyce's authorial voice using long Latinate words which do not have any place in Bloom's own vocabulary. These passages need to be read slowly to tease out their meaning and hence their comic effect.

867 *In what final satisfaction did these antagonistic sentiments and reflections, reduced to their simplest forms converge?* In the same style, the narrator notes Leopold's satisfaction with what we realise are the twin hemispheres of Molly's bottom. He has a mild erection and kisses them. This is far as their sexual interaction will go tonight. Molly stirs and wakes; sleepily, she asks her husband for an account of his day's activities. He tells her what he has been doing, with a certain amount of censorship, where necessary. He emphasises the importance of his meeting and friendship with Stephen Dedalus, *professor and author.*

869 The narrator observes that during this conversation they both have things on their minds; Molly is aware that they have not had full intercourse for over 10 years – since a few weeks before the death of their baby son, Rudy. Leopold, describing his travels round the city is

aware that, since their daughter Milly's first period, both women have conspired to interrogate him about his activities and hence limit his freedom.

At last, they both settle down to sleep; Bloom lying with his head at the foot of the bed.

Their relative positions are described as if on a map of the world. We are reminded that they are being carried through space by the motion of the earth.

Molly is fulfilled, recumbent, full of seed. She is Gea-Tellus (the earth mother). Leopold is curled up in the foetal position.

Womb? Weary? He has travelled.

He is drowsily murmuring to himself, variations on the words *Sinbad the Sailor* (another traveller). He will soon be asleep.

Notes on Episode 18: PENELOPE (871-933)

This episode is called 'Penelope' after the wife of Ulysses, who waited many years, besieged by suitors, for her husband to come home from the Trojan Wars.

Joyce's Penelope is Molly Bloom who has waited all day for her husband to come home, but, unlike the Greek Penelope, she has not remained faithful. Molly is 33 and her husband is 38.

The episode is all voiced by Molly as she lies in bed, with Leopold sleeping upside down beside her. Her mind is very active, with her thoughts all running into each other. She thinks about the past days and the ones to come; her relationships with her husband; her daughter Milly; her lover, Blazes Boylan, with whom she was having sex a few hours ago, and her previous admirers. There are more distant memories of growing up in Gibraltar where her father served in the British army. She recalls her early passion for Bloom and their courtship and married life together. She muses about sexuality, menstruation and childbirth. There seem to be no pauses and no punctuation!

In fact there are eight 'sentences', but (in our edition) only one full stop, right at the end. The other sentences just break off and the next one begins with an indented line. It might help to pencil in the number at the beginning (indent) of each sentence.

We tend to look for full stops when reading and hurry towards each one as a resting place. Without any, you may at first feel lost. My advice is to read slowly, one phrase at a time, to take in in the sense.

This is how the episode starts:

SENTENCE 1 (871 – 880)
Yes because he never did a thing like that before as to ask to get his breakfast in bed...

Molly's first thoughts are about Bloom's goodnight request. Is he pretending to be ill?

She thinks he did this once before to make himself interesting to Mrs Riordan, their former landlady, in the hope that Mrs R might leave them something in her will. But she likes that he is polite to old women and waiters and beggars. What would she do if he was really ill? *Men are so weak and puling when theyre sick they want a woman to get well if his nose bleeds youd think it was O tragic* (872)

Lower down, note the thought: *yes he came somewhere Im sure by his appetite.*

Molly is sure that Bloom has had sex during the day and wonders with whom.

(Actually, it was with himself.) Was he making up lies about how he spent the day? Or was he with *some little bitch* (line 7). She remembers him *scribbling something a letter* and guiltily covering it up with blotting paper to hide it from her. Was he writing to some woman trying to make a fool out of him? (see episode 5). He did get rather keen on a maid they once had (Mary in Ontario Terrace) and Molly had to give her a week's notice, nominally for stealing some oysters.

He must do it somewhere (874). Their marital sex has been unsatisfactory since the death of their infant son 10 years ago (now the most he will do is just come on her bottom). She remembers Boylan squeezing her hand as she and Bloom walked together with him one evening by the Tolka (one of Dublin's rivers).

We are now near the bottom of 874 and Molly is fantasising about paying for sex *with a nice looking boy*. On 875 she goes back to memories of walking out with Bloom. *Who tired me out with statues* and again regrets there's no satisfaction for the woman in marital sex. But she does find kissing exciting.

As a young girl, she had to make her confession to Father Corrigan. *he touched me father and what harm if he did where and I said on the canal bank like a fool but whereabouts on your person my child;* She used to rather fancy Father Corrigan.

Sometimes when she says 'he' it's hard to know which man she is referring to. When in doubt, it's usually Bloom, for whom she still has a lot of affection,

But (876, line 6) when she says: *I wonder was he satisfied with me* she is remembering her afternoon tryst with Blazes Boylan. He is the one who slapped her behind in such a vulgar way. She wonders if he's dreaming about her now; who gave him the flower and what was the drink he smelt of? After the *port and potted meat* she fell asleep till that *thunder woke me up as if the world was coming to an end.*

877 she has vivid memories of sex with Boylan. *He must have come 3 or 4 times with that tremendous red brute of his.* And *what's the idea of making us like that with a big hole in the middle of us...* She thinks about how women are constantly getting pregnant and having one child after another. She wonders about risking another pregnancy. Having Boylan's child? *Poldy has more spunk in him* (Poldy is her pet name for Leopold). She drifts on to imagining that Bloom must have been aroused by his encounter in the street

with Josie Powell, now Mrs Breen, an old flame and one-time rival, and of course, thinking about Molly and Boylan having sex. Her jealousy of Josie is revived (last line 877). She remembers *the night of Georgina Simpson's housewarming*, before she and Bloom were married. That night she felt very jealous of him dancing and sitting out with Josie. She would easily be able to tell if he was seeing Josie again; and we realise how fiercely Molly cares for him still. Molly used to confide in Josie until she and Bloom were married.

879 (bottom of page) Now poor Josie is married to Mr Breen (*that dotty husband of hers*) who used to go to bed with his muddy boots on. Molly thinks she is much better off with Bloom, who always wipes his feet when he comes in. *of course hed never find another woman like me to put up with him the way I do* (middle of 880). She thinks about the notorious Mrs Maybrick who had been tried in London, a few years earlier, for allegedly murdering her husband with poison. She was convicted but escaped hanging.

The first sentence tails off with *surely are they* (5th line from the bottom) and the next one begins, with an indent, on the following line: *theyre all so different*

SENTENCE 2 (880 -891)

880 four lines from bottom: *theyre all so different*...Molly is thinking about her sex with Boylan; but, characteristically, her attention moves seamlessly to other men: Bloom in the early days of their courtship and more recently as a husband; young Lieutenant Gardner who was her first boyfriend when she was a young girl growing up in Gibraltar and who

sadly died of enteric fever in the Boer War; Bartell d'Arcy, the tenor (and fellow artiste).

880-881 Boylan admiring her foot in the DBC (the Dublin Bakery Company café). Bloom also has a thing about her feet: wanting her to take her stockings off or being turned on by her muddy boots.

881-2 Being kissed by Bartell d'Arcy (a real person) on the choir stairs after singing Ave Maria. Then on to Bloom's fascination with her drawers (underpants) or indeed any woman's underwear; and his surreptitious outings on his own.

883 More about drawers. Bloom asking her lift her orange petticoat in the street or he would go down on his knees to look. How she touched the front of his trousers just as she did with Gardner (see above); how Bloom wrote her a letter *with all those words in it*. She declined his proposal but wasn't offended.

884 More about Bloom who sent her 8 poppies on her birthday. And *kissed my heart at Dolphins barn* (a Dublin suburb). Then suddenly *(I hope hell come on Monday)* Molly is back to Boylan and hoping he won't let her down. She doesn't like people calling unexpectedly (like Professor Goodwin). At first she thought Boylan was not going to keep his appointment at 4 p.m. She will be going to Belfast with him to sing in a concert. Fortunately Bloom will have to go to Ennis that day for the anniversary of his father's death.

885 An episode with Bloom on a train when he insisted on taking his soup into the carriage and embarrassed

her. She hopes she will travel 1st Class on the train with Boylan. Might they be naughty in the tunnels? Suppose they eloped? Memories of other concerts.

886 Bloom's antics at concerts and in politics. More about Stanley Gardner, Molly's lost soldier-boy love. Fine-looking soldiers on parade in Gibraltar.

887 She imagines the fun of going shopping in Belfast with Boylan. She had better leave her wedding ring behind. But does he really like her? Memories of sex with Boylan: He's too heavy; he should put it in from behind like Mr Mastiansky with his wife. He's well dressed; he got into rage, tearing up his betting tickets and swearing after Lenehan's tip failed to win. Lenehan was *making free* with Molly after the Glencree (Lord Mayor's) dinner, on the way back in the coach (See Episode 10, Wandering Rocks)

888 Memories of the Lord Mayor's dinner. *I want at least two other chemises* (from Boylan). What sort of drawers does he like? (Probably he prefers a woman to be without them.) Problems buying underwear. Maybe she should lose some weight.

889 Did Bloom remember to get her some more of that face lotion? Worries about her skin; wishes she had more money to spend on good clothes; she is nearly 33 and her youth will only last till she's 35. (Actually she is nearly 34). Some older women seem to be able to keep their looks.

890 Men are all made one way (*only a black man I'd like to try*). Her thoughts ramble over Lily Langtry and

the Prince of Wales; the semi-pornographic books Leopold has bought her and back to Lily Langtry and her affair with royalty. Molly thinks Bloom ought to give up his job at the *Freeman* newspaper (where he only gets commission) and get something that pays regularly.

891 She remembers how he lost his job with Hely's the stationer. Molly tried to patch it up with the boss, Mr Cuffe, who clearly fancied her; but she lost her confidence, aware of the rottenness of her dress. She only bought it to please Bloom. She should have gone to a different shop. She hates going to rich shops and if she takes Leopold he is really no help at all. Mr Cuffe had looked very hard at her chest when they were leaving *I just half smiled I know my chest was out that way at the door when he said Im extremely sorry and Im sure you were*

SENTENCE 3 (892-894)

892 first line: *yes I think he made them a bit firmer sucking them like that...* Molly is considering her breasts after Boylan has sucked them. She compares them with men's genitals. Poldy once suggested she could *pose naked for some rich fellow* when they were short of money after he lost his job at Hely's. Would she be like the picture of a naked nymph that Bloom hung up in their bedroom? Men keep trying to expose themselves to her in the street (especially soldiers of the Cameron Highlanders).

893-4 Molly remembers sheltering from the cold in a men's public toilet. Aren't men afraid of their external genitals being damaged? She thinks again about some of Bloom's irritating ways: using long words (j*awbreakers*) to explain things to her; burning the frying pan while cooking his breakfast kidney; more about her breasts: Boylan bit one of them; with Milly her breasts were swollen with milk; Bloom sucked them to relieve her and then wanted to *milk me into the tea* (Bloom always has practical ideas). Now she is missing Boylan again. She remembers how it felt (*I was coming for about 5 minutes with my legs round him*). He's a *savage brute* – but she is counting the days till Monday when he will call again for more of the same.

SENTENCE 4 (894 -900)

894 (indented line 13) *frseeeeeeefronnnng* is the sound of a train whistle. The lives of the engine drivers and their wives. *Loves old sweet sonnnng* is one of her favourite concert pieces. It is also known as 'Just a Song at Twilight' We'll hear more of this 'theme-song' in Sentence 5. It's good to listen to the CD performance to appreciate its haunting effect.

This sentence is largely about Molly's memories of her girlhood in Gibraltar where her father (Major Tweedy) was a serving soldier.

895-7 She had a married, slightly older, friend called Hester Stanhope, of whom she has fond recollections. Hester wrote her letters when she was in Paris. *Doggerina* was her nick-name for Molly; she calls her own (older) husband *wogger*. Molly thinks sadly of the happy times she enjoyed with Hester. Although the bullfight was gruesome and cruel. On the night of the storm she slept in Hester's bed. Life in Gibraltar became very dull after the Stanhopes finally left. Hester gave her novels to read, although she doesn't like *books with a Molly in them* (Moll Flanders) She remembers watching the Stanhopes' ship sailing away. *she kissed me six or seven times didn't I cry yes… it got as dull as the devil after they went.* Gibraltar after that seemed to be nothing but military parades, ceremonies, guns going off and her father talking with Captain Groves about old battles.

898 She was so bored, she wrote letters to herself. And so, to recent times in Dublin. An attractive, but unresponsive medical student in Holles Street. The country farmers at the cattle sales were stupid too.

899-900 More about letters. She imagines an exchange of love letters with Boylan. Sentence 4 ends at line 6, p 900 *:ash pit*

SENTENCE 5 (900 – 906)

900-902 *Mulveys was the first…*This sentence is largely about Lieutenant Mulvey, Molly's first admirer in Gibraltar. Mrs Rubio was the housekeeper. Mulvey followed her along *the calle Real* and wrote her first love letter signed *an admirer.*

There is a flower that bloometh is a song made famous by the Irish tenor John McCormack (1884-1945).

Cappoquin he came from: Mulvey says he comes from Cappoquin a town in Ireland on the Blackwater river. He left Gibraltar in May.

There is a digression about the naughtiness of the Barbary Apes on the Rock of Gibraltar which leads to memories of Molly and Mulvey's first walk together at the firtree cove and their adolescent lovemaking. She can't at first remember his given name (Harry).

903 She wondered if he would ever come back and marry her. Maybe he is now married to someone else. Marriage makes her think of her own husband and being 'Mrs Bloom'.

904 More memories of fun with Harry Mulvey in Gibraltar. He gave her *that clumsy Claddagh ring* that she subsequently gave to his successor, Lieutenant Gardner, who died of dysentery in South Africa.

Bottom of page 904 Molly hears the whistle *Frseeeeeeeeeeeeeeeeeeeefrong* as another train comes by. Its weeping tone evokes a line from 'Love's Old Sweet Song': *once in the dear dead days beyond recall* and she rehearses how she will sing it (in Belfast with Boylan).

905-906 *ere oer the mists began I hate that istsbeg* ' Istsbeg' is the difficult transition for the singer: ***mists – beg****an*.

She expresses her contempt for the younger singers and their lower social status *soldiers daughter I am*. Her thoughts flit rapidly to Gardner, then having a husband and daughter, unlike those younger girls; then to pride in having captivated a virile lover like Boylan – and back to the forthcoming vocal performance *(deep down chin back not too much make it double.)* What else will she sing? What shall she wear? She wants to pass some wind but doesn't want to wake Poldy: and manages it quietly.

SENTENCE 6 (906 – 915)

906-7 *that was a relief*...Memories of a cold winter in Gibraltar when she was about 10.
 Last two lines: *those medicals leading him astray again.* This, of course, is about Bloom coming in late. Home life with husband and the cat… Tomorrow's food shopping. Plans for a picnic with Boylan.

908 A rather alarming boat trip on the sea at Bray with Bloom pretending he could row. *That other beauty Burke*: this refers to 'Pisser' Burke, who is on the list of her suitors in 'Ithaca' but clearly one of the unsuccessful ones. Books Poldy buys her. The sea at Gibraltar and the fishermen. She doesn't like being alone in this big house.

909 Bloom's plans for the house and for holidays. He is always making plans that come to nothing. Leaving her alone all day: fears of being murdered by an intruder. Now Milly is away too.

910-11 Did Bloom send Milly away to learn photography *on account of me and Boylan.* Molly's complaints and worries about Milly's rapidly developing sexuality. She and Molly were both moved by the performance of Martin Harvey, the actor, as Sidney Carton in an adaptation of *A Tale of Two Cities.*

912 *suppose there are few men like that left.* Bloom's father's suicide. More angry thoughts about Milly's

impudence and rudeness *I gave her 2 fine cracks across the ear for that.* It's Bloom's fault *for having the two of us here slaving* and not getting in a servant. The present one, Mrs Fleming, is too old and frail.

913 More complaints about Bloom. She objects to him bringing his friends home (*and a dog if you please that might have been mad*). She doesn't like Simon Dedalus. Bloom shouldn't have climbed over the railings to get in and risked tearing *a big hole in his grand funeral trousers.* Now, Molly is feeling aggrieved over just about everything, especially men.

And then: *wait O Jesus wait yes that thing has come on me.* Her period has started. It must have been the vigorous sex. Will Boylan mind? *Will he like it? Some men do.*

914 Memories of a period coming on in a theatre box while Bloom was talking about Spinoza. The flow increases (*its pouring out of me like the sea*). The loose quoits on the bed were jingling so much with their weight, she had them move down to the floor.

915 Molly gets on the chamber pot and remembers how she sat on Boylan's knee last night. She admires her own thighs. She starts to pass urine (noisily) as well as blood: *O how the waters come down at Lahore*

SENTENCE 7 (915 – 923)

915-16 (middle) *who knows is there anything the matter.* Molly is worried about her frequent periods and she remembers going to see a gynaecologist (Dr Collins). This was before she was married and Bloom was writing her passionate letters which turned her on. When they first met they stared at each other for 10 minutes.

917 Bloom's strange habits and requests: wanting her to sing a classy song, talking to her about religion and persecution; kneeling to use the toilet; sleeping *at the foot of the bed* (head downwards); showing her a statue of an Indian god in the Kildare Street museum. The old press creaks when she takes out a sanitary towel but Bloom doesn't wake. *Hes sleeping hard had a good time somewhere still she must have given him great value for his money*

918 The lumpy old bed *Here we are as bad as ever after 16 years after how many houses.* They are always having to move house or getting evicted. Bloom keeps losing his job by doing something stupid, just when things have started to go well.

More complaints about him coming in at 2 a.m. and climbing over the area wall and (she thinks), having a secret affair.

Bottom line: *Aristocrats Masterpiece.* She means Aristotle's book with (919) illustrations of abnormal babies: *rotten pictures children with two heads.* The complaints go on: Bloom's demand for breakfast in bed; his inept attempt at cunnilingus (*thinking only of his own pleasure his tongue is too flat).*

Who did he go with last night? Could it have been Josie Breen? *Or some little bitch hes got.*

He keeps *throwing his sheeps eyes* (ogling) women. *Those two on skirt duty* must have been prostitutes. He spends money with his disreputable friends

920 (middle) *well theyre not going to get my husband again into their clutches*. Molly is actually praising Bloom now because *he has sense enough not to squander every penny piece* but *looks after his wife and family*. She thinks about the late Paddy Dignam leaving his wife and 5 children in poverty. Then back to that Glencree dinner when Ben Dollard *(base barreltone)* borrowed a swallowtail (dress suit) of which the trousers were embarrassingly tight round his genitals.

921 Simon Dedalus and Bartell d'Arcy were also 'flirtyfying' singers. (Both of them have fancied her in the past.)

Simon was married to May Goulding (sister of Ritchie Goulding, the lawyer, who had dinner with Bloom in the Sirens episode.) Now he's a widower and she wonders *what sort is his son*: Bloom has told her about bringing Stephen Dedalus back for cocoa and his plans for her to give him singing lessons. She remembers seeing Stephen as a little boy. Will he find her attractive? The cards this morning seemed to predict a meeting with *a young stranger*.

922 She dreamed about poetry last night. Will she be too old for Stephen? At least he's not too stuck up to sit in the kitchen and have cocoa with Bloom.

I hope hes not a professor like Goodwin was he was a patent professor of John Jameson

(John Jameson is a brand of Irish whiskey.)

They all write about some woman in their poetry (So Stephen will write about Molly.)

923 Molly thinks dreamily about handsome young men bathing naked. She would like to kiss that lovely little statue and suck his cock. *If only I can get in with a handsome young poet at my age.* She will see if the cards predict that it will happen. She will teach him what he doesn't know about love and sex until he feels faint. When his writing becomes famous and writes about her publicly she will be famous too: *our 2 photographs in all the papers*

The sentence ends with *O but then what am I going to do about him though.* Him of course is her husband!

SENTENCE 8 (923- 933)

923-4 No *that's no way for him has he no manners* Molly is thinking about Boylan's rough rudeness. Perhaps he couldn't help slapping her buttocks because they are so round and white. She wished she was a man herself for a change so she could enjoy a woman's body as they do. Naughty rhymes with double-entendres. Men can pick and choose any woman they please while women are chained up by jealous husbands. She wishes they could all be friends instead of getting upset about adultery.

925 *Fair Tyrants*: the title of a one of those lurid novels Bloom bought her. Why is he so cold to her? *A woman wants to be embraced 20 times a day* (but not kissed on the impersonal bottom). She considers wild ideas of finding a sailor or a gipsy as a lover; or someone in a *silk hat like that KC lives up somewhere.* (A KC is a King's Counsel. Same as a QC when the sovereign is female).

926 line 6: *O move over your big carcase* Bloom is taking more than his fair share of the bed.

Don Poldo de la Flora Molly invents an ironic title for 'Poldy'. More complaints about Bloom and men in general. The world would be better if women were in charge.

I suppose hes running wild now She moves smoothly on to Stephen whose mother has died. Why was I unable to have a son, she wonders, painfully.

927 Thinking sadly about poor little Rudy. Then back to Stephen (*I wonder why he wouldn't stay the night).* (We readers have to be quick to catch these sudden switches of subject.)

Women are not so admirable after all (*we are a dreadful lot of bitches)*

Wondering about Stephen's unusual surname (Dedalus) In Gibraltar there were people with very strange names.

928 Fantasies about having Stephen to stay: mutual language teaching, making meals for him, introducing herself; he could have Molly's room; Bloom could make breakfast for both of them; she would need some new clothes.

3rd line from bottom: *Ill just give him one more chance* Now Molly is thinking of Bloom again.

929 She might go to the market for some nice fresh food for him; She will try to please him: *Ill go about rather gay not too much singing.* She plots the seduction of her husband using a tempting breakfast, and arousing state of undress – even trying to arouse his jealousy by taunting him with an account of sex

with Boylan. God must have wanted a woman to be sexy *or He wouldn't have made us the way He did so attractive to men.* If all else fails, she will offer him her bottom including its hole – and then ask him for some money to buy underclothes.

930 line 11 *O wait now sonny my turn is coming:* Molly will want him (probably anticipating Boylan's next visit) to give her a climax too. But then she realises that she has forgotten her period (*this bloody pest of a thing)*.
his omission (line 18) she means 'emission'.
Molly's thoughts turn to the time of night, what different people (e.g. in China) are doing. She needs to get up early to get some flowers *in case he brings him* (Stephen) *home again tomorrow*

931 More about entertaining Stephen; a rhapsody about nature *the wild mountains then the sea.* How can people say there is no God? *why don't they go and create something?*
Then, the last reverie, the end of Molly's soliloquy and the end of *Ulysses:* she remembers the day Bloom proposed to her:
The day we were lying among the rhododendrons at Howth's head (the northern promontory of Dublin Bay). The long kiss; the mouth-to-mouth transfer of seed cake; the romantic things he said; a flurry of thoughts about her Gibraltar days and Lieutenant Mulvey (*he kissed me under the Moorish wall).* We are somewhat dismayed that Mulvey should be the man in her thoughts at a moment like this – but no – *as well him as another* – Molly is surely back, where she

belongs with Bloom in the famously affirmative last words ending in *yes I said yes I will Yes.*

Footnote: When Joyce's wife, Nora, was asked for her opinion about her husband's achievement in writing this chapter entirely from the female point of view, she replied, 'Jim knows nothing at all about women.'